The Arcturian Code
Crystals of Healing and Harmony
Luiz Santos

Copyright © 2023 Luiz Santos
All rights reserved.
No part of this book may be reproduced in any form or by any means without written permission from the copyright holder.
Cover image © Orbis Studio
Review by Marco Avelar
Graphic design by Tania Navarro
Layout by Paulo Xavier
All rights reserved to:
Luiz A. Santos
Category: Holism

Summary

Prologue 5
Chapter 1 Arcturian Crystals... 8
Chapter 2 Origin and Frequency 13
Chapter 3 Preparing to Work with Crystals 19
Chapter 4 Purifying and Activating Crystals 25
Chapter 5 Healing Energy and Properties................................... 31
Chapter 6 Connection with the Frequency................................. 38
Chapter 7 Energy Shield 45
Chapter 8 Energy Harmony 51
Chapter 9 Crystal Meditation Techniques 58
Chapter 10 Chakra Alignment 65
Chapter 11 Emotional and Mental Healing................................. 71
Chapter 12 Physical Healing.. 78
Chapter 13 Energetic Cleansing of Spaces 85
Chapter 14 Creating Protection Grids... 92
Chapter 15 Spiritual Awakening and Higher Connection 99
Chapter 16 Strengthening Intuition... 106
Chapter 17 Desire Manifestation 113
Chapter 18 Sacred Space.. 120
Chapter 19 Purification Rituals.. 127
Chapter 20 Strengthening the Energetic Field 134
Chapter 21 Energizing Crystals 142
Chapter 22 Protection Against Negative Energies.................... 150
Chapter 23 Moments of Transition and Change 157

Chapter 24 Self-Confidence 164
Chapter 25 Consciousness Expansion 172
Chapter 26 Inner Balance 179
Chapter 27 Deep Meditation 186
Chapter 28 Spiritual Protection 194
Chapter 29 Advanced Healing Techniques 202
Chapter 30 Personal Journey 210
Chapter 31 Crystal Integration 218
Epilogue 226

Prologue

There is an ancient, pulsing, invisible energy that surrounds you at this very moment. A force that goes beyond what the eyes can see and what logic can grasp. An energy not of this world, yet resonating in frequencies that touch the core of your existence. Like a subtle calling, it arrives to you, traveling across galaxies and distant times, concentrated in a near-magical form: the Arcturian crystals. These crystals are living portals, transmitters of a cosmic frequency—a silent melody that resonates with the essence of harmony and healing.

These crystals, which you are about to discover, are not merely shining rocks. Each one holds the signature of galactic wisdom, a resonance that links you directly to the universe and the profound knowledge of the Arcturians. Keepers of ancient knowledge, these crystals await to reveal what is subtle and powerful within. They vibrate with a presence as ancient as the cosmos, an energy that knows no bounds of time or space and manifests in your life now as an opportunity for transformation.

Do you feel in tune with this inexplicable attraction? There is a part of you that intuits this connection, recognizing this moment as synchronicity, as something that simply "must be." These crystals transcend expectations, surpassing the borders of usual comprehension. By opening yourself to them, you access a frequency that activates the deepest centers of being, aligning not only body and mind but the very essence of your energy with what is truly eternal.

Each of these crystals holds a unique energetic signature, an almost imperceptible yet undeniable pulse that reverberates through your energy field, echoing the truths and healing you seek. By holding them, by connecting with their vibration, you will notice they have a silent presence that, more than speaking, listens. They invite you to dive into your own depths, exploring inner territories you may have never dared to visit. This is the journey these crystals propose: a return to the self, an expansion that goes beyond the bounds of usual understanding.

The Arcturians, those who infused their essence into these crystals, are not just beings from another galaxy but guides with spiritual wisdom that encompasses balance, peace, and protection. In a world full of noise and distractions, they remind us of silence, serenity, and intuition. These crystals hold in them waves of healing that can protect you from external influences, from the invisible forces that drain your vitality. It's not only protection they offer but also a serenity that embraces, that welcomes, and reminds you of who you are beyond the layers of the everyday.

And it's not only about protection. It is about rediscovering something vast and, at the same time, intimate. These crystals, when used, become an extension of your energy, a reflection of your purest intentions. The more you open yourself, the more you allow them to tune your field, the more intensely you will experience this rare state of peace and unity. You will feel a frequency that is not imposed but rather awakened, a gentle wave that harmonizes and guides every cell, every thought, every emotion.

Imagine the power of being free from the invisible tensions that hold you back, from anxieties that accompany you without explanation. With these crystals, your energy begins to align so naturally that the noise disappears, the dense dissolves, and lightness takes over. The feeling of peace and clarity is not fleeting; it is a deep transformation arising from resonance with something beyond yourself, an almost tangible presence that leads you to experience your essence in a state of balance.

Throughout this journey, these crystals will become more than mere tools. They will guide you beyond the veil that separates the known from the unknown, revealing fragments of wisdom that you already carry but have been dormant. With every interaction, you will be building a relationship, a partnership that respects and responds to your intentions. And as you allow this connection, you will realize they are not inanimate objects; they are living companions, a presence that listens and responds, creating an energetic dance that expands your field and elevates your frequency.

By allowing this frequency to become part of your life, each crystal will act as a bridge, connecting your earthly existence to a space where energy flows freely, where intuition strengthens, and peace expands. This is not a fleeting experience but a path to continuous transformation. Each moment with these crystals draws you closer to the essence of who you are and who you can become.

Chapter 1
Arcturian Crystals

There exists a remarkable facet of the universe, concealed within shimmering gems that hold an ancient, unearthly essence—the Arcturian crystals. These crystalline structures are more than simple stones; they embody a frequency—a signature vibration, if you will—that links directly to the Arcturian energy, a force beyond the limits of typical human experience. Arcturians, extraterrestrial beings of a profound spiritual nature, are said to impart energies of protection, healing, and wisdom, energies that these crystals preserve with silent, enduring potency. From the depths of galaxies far from our own, these stones traveled, drawn by purpose to a place where their potential might be activated. These crystals are unique in the cosmic spectrum, unlike any earthly stone, not merely because of their composition but for the frequency they carry—a resonance born of light and energy.

For those who can connect to the subtle vibrations of the Arcturian frequency, these crystals serve as powerful conduits for healing and personal transformation. Arcturian energy is described as a harmonizing force, one that transcends conventional concepts of time, space, and matter. It is often felt as an undulating pulse or a sensation of profound warmth and calmness, reaching deep within to heal, harmonize, and align. Some describe it as stepping into a realm where peace is more than a feeling; it is a state of being. The frequency of these crystals is no accident. Embedded within them is an intrinsic property—an unyielding tether to the Arcturian vibrational state, an ancient, nurturing quality that holds protection and healing in its very essence.

With these crystals, those attuned to their presence are said to access a frequency that transcends the dimensions of the physical and moves directly into the spiritual. This connection is not something to take lightly. To work with these crystals is to enter into a conscious relationship, a two-way exchange where intention is met with the potential for profound healing and spiritual growth. Yet, as with any journey into the unseen, it requires trust, respect, and a willingness to listen. For in these stones lies not just a wellspring of power, but a deep wisdom—the silent song of the stars that only those who listen with open hearts can hear.

When utilized in healing practices, the crystals are revered for their unique vibrational signatures, which resonate at frequencies that interact directly with the body's energy centers. They serve as protective talismans, strengthening the user's energetic field against any form of imbalance or negative influence. This shielding is delicate yet potent; it does not obstruct but rather strengthens and harmonizes, offering a layer of serenity that permeates through to the soul. For practitioners, working with these crystals requires a form of surrender—a quieting of the mind to tune into the crystalline frequency and align with the energy it emanates.

In use, Arcturian crystals have an almost magnetic pull. Their function is less about force and more about alignment, acting as quiet harmonizers, vibrating with an energy that encourages the spirit to match its own frequency to the crystal's. It's as though the user's energy is drawn into an unseen chord, resonating with the unseen, healing light of Arcturian influence. Those who hold these stones often report feeling a sense of protection, as if wrapped in a gentle shield, a peace that stems from the heart of the universe itself.

Indeed, one could say the true importance of working with Arcturian crystals lies in understanding the mutual exchange of energy. When held with conscious intent, they become more than stones; they transform into partners, attuning not just to the user's energy but amplifying it, realigning it to match the harmonious frequency of the Arcturian current. Through focus and presence, these crystals invite one into a cosmic symphony, a song that transcends the physical realm and resonates through all layers of existence.

The science of Arcturian crystals is veiled in mystery yet remarkably detailed in its explanation. Unlike earthly gemstones, whose energies and effects are well-documented within the realms of mineralogy and metaphysics, Arcturian crystals defy conventional understanding. They are intricate constructions of matter and energy, born not from the geological processes of planets but shaped by the stars' radiance and the vastness of cosmic dust. These crystals are unique structures that seem to carry intelligence, attuned to a frequency outside our dimension, crafted with an intentional design to serve as conduits of the Arcturian energy signature.

The nature of this signature is worth examining, for Arcturian crystals contain more than just trace minerals or molecular patterns. These crystals resonate at specific frequencies, a precise energetic wavelength that allows them to absorb, store, and transmit what is known as the Arcturian current. This frequency is subtle yet intense, a delicate web of energy that links them to the source of Arcturian knowledge and healing. Where earthly stones may align to the frequencies of the planet, its minerals, and elements, Arcturian crystals transcend these constraints. Their structure is alive with the Arcturian resonance, humming with a force that can only be described as otherworldly.

These crystals, when held or worked with, open a channel, almost like an energetic gateway that allows one to experience the essence of Arcturian guidance, protection, and healing. Users often report feeling an immediate shift upon contact, a sense that the crystal is actively responding to their energy. Those familiar with traditional crystal healing practices may sense the distinction quickly; Arcturian crystals not only absorb and amplify energy but possess an inherent intelligence that seems to understand the intention behind the user's interaction. For many practitioners, this quality is a testament to the complexity of Arcturian stones, whose layers resonate deeply with the vibrations of higher consciousness.

These crystals operate in distinct ways from conventional stones. Practitioners and crystal enthusiasts alike attest that Arcturian stones act as direct channels, inviting energy to flow through them rather than acting solely as containers or amplifiers. In healing practices, they are known to tune into specific energetic frequencies tailored to the individual's needs, whether that be physical healing, emotional stability, or spiritual protection. They do not indiscriminately transmit energy; instead, they seem to intuitively respond to the subtleties of the user's energy field, enhancing what is most beneficial at that moment. This characteristic has led to a growing interest among healers, many of whom testify to the crystal's transformative effects.

Accounts from users of Arcturian crystals are many and varied. Some describe feeling an aura of profound calm that emanates from these stones, enveloping them as though wrapped in the light of distant stars. Others feel a warmth that radiates from the core of the crystal, pulsing in time with their heartbeat, as though syncing their energy with the rhythm of the universe. A few have even reported visions—flashes of insight, cosmic vistas, moments of spiritual revelation. These experiences, while diverse, share a common thread: the feeling of being guided, of stepping into a stream of wisdom beyond time, a vast reservoir of light from the Arcturian realm.

Such testimonials highlight the distinction of Arcturian crystals, for their effects often touch more than the individual's physical senses. Users report emotional healing that feels profound and deeply seated, as if untangling knots from the very fabric of their being. Healers working with Arcturian crystals have recounted the way these stones create a powerful resonance within the auric field, fortifying it against negativity and bringing a sense of clarity and protection. Indeed, these crystals act not just as tools but as allies—energy partners that shift and guide the spirit toward a higher state of alignment.

For the uninitiated, this concept of crystals possessing "intention" or "intelligence" may seem far-fetched. Yet those who work consistently with Arcturian stones describe them not as inert objects, but as living, vibrant extensions of the Arcturian energy itself. Their effect is more than metaphoric; it's a lived experience, a subtle shift in the energy around and within, perceptible to those attuned to its call. And so, while each Arcturian crystal holds a single frequency, they act as keys that unlock layers of understanding, guiding the user toward the unknown dimensions of self-awareness.

In every sense, Arcturian crystals seem to pulse with a wisdom that is rare, an energy imbued with purpose and profound intent. Through them, one might sense a doorway to the Arcturian world, a realm where boundaries dissolve and healing becomes a harmonious song, woven by the light and essence of another galaxy. For the seekers who resonate with this energy, these crystals serve as companions on their journey, guiding them gently yet powerfully toward deeper realms of healing, insight, and protection. The testimonials serve as affirmations of this relationship, reminders that the crystals act not merely as instruments, but as wise, knowing presences awaiting discovery.

Chapter 2
Origin and Frequency

To speak of Arcturian crystals is to trace a story that begins far beyond Earth, deep within the embrace of star-strewn realms where matter and light dance in harmony. These crystals, formed under the distant influence of Arcturian energy, are unlike anything shaped by the pressures of Earth's crust. They resonate with a frequency that's not just cosmic but transcendent, vibrating with the subtle hum of Arcturian wisdom—a force that bridges vast distances to reach us, carrying with it the quiet pulse of healing and enlightenment.

It's believed that these stones were first introduced to humanity through the silent calling of Arcturian guides, who, through dreams, visions, and subtle whispers, guided seekers to uncover the crystals hidden in the earth's folds. This history binds the crystals not only to the stars but to the seekers who are drawn to their energy. Each crystal is a relic of the Arcturian light, shaped through eons and infused with an energy that transcends the concept of time, a reminder of the unity between human consciousness and the far reaches of the cosmos. Those who hold these stones understand that they are not mere objects but connectors to a frequency that ripples through the unseen.

In working with these crystals, one may begin to feel the resonance that Arcturian guides communicate through—a language of energy and frequency. The essence of Arcturian energy is one of elevated compassion, a vibration that, unlike the denser frequencies encountered in earthly life, seems to soar into the realms of purity and light. This frequency is not just a concept; it is a sensation, a presence felt on an intrinsic level, reaching deep within the user and initiating a transformation that aligns the physical with the spiritual. The process of connecting with this frequency feels, to many, like stepping into a flow of stillness and clarity, where one's inner and outer worlds come into a gentle, harmonious alignment.

At the heart of this interaction lies the principle of energetic absorption and transmission, the means by which Arcturian crystals communicate their resonance. When a practitioner holds one of these stones, they are not merely connecting to the crystal itself but to the Arcturian energy it embodies. The crystal acts as a vessel, absorbing the energy from the surrounding environment, from the practitioner's intentions, and, most importantly, from the Arcturian source itself. It's a relationship built on exchange; the crystal receives energy, holds it, and, in turn, shares it with the user, allowing for a harmonious flow that enhances and purifies the practitioner's own frequency.

Those who work with these stones often describe the frequency as one that initiates a gentle, yet profound, opening. The energy transmitted by the crystal penetrates beyond the physical senses, entering into the layers of the auric field, the chakras, and even the subtler layers of the human consciousness. In this way, Arcturian crystals go beyond merely amplifying energy; they transform it, guiding it into alignment with the higher frequencies of Arcturian consciousness. And for those who open themselves to this exchange, there is a sense of grounding and balance that feels almost otherworldly, as though touching a hidden dimension within oneself.

This process of energy absorption is both complex and delicately balanced, for the crystals not only absorb energy from their surroundings but actively filter it, ensuring that only the frequencies aligned with healing and spiritual upliftment are retained. The crystals seem to possess an innate wisdom that discerns the energies that are beneficial from those that may disrupt the user's natural state. This ability to selectively absorb is a rare quality, suggesting that the crystals are not merely passive objects but are attuned to an intelligence that transcends their form. Through their filtering process, they shield their user, creating a barrier against lower frequencies, a subtle yet powerful layer of protection that keeps the spirit and the energy field clean and clear.

In holistic practices, the use of these crystals for energy absorption and transmission has gained deep respect. Healers working with Arcturian crystals often report that the stones seem to enhance the flow of energy during sessions, acting as conduits that bring both practitioner and recipient into alignment with the Arcturian vibration. Their frequency is not overpowering, but rather a subtle, guiding presence that supports the healing journey, weaving an invisible thread that links healer, crystal, and patient in a single energetic exchange. Through this process, the Arcturian energy transmitted by the crystals uplifts, balances, and restores, creating an experience of wholeness that resonates deeply within the body and mind.

The power of these crystals lies not only in their ability to heal but in the quality of connection they provide—a bridge between the earthly and the cosmic. As the crystals absorb the practitioner's intention, they amplify it and resonate with the Arcturian frequency, creating a wave of energy that flows outward, touching everything in its path. For those who seek to attune themselves to this energy, the crystals act as a guiding light, a reminder that within each of us is the potential to align with frequencies far beyond our own, to reach out and become part of the vast, interconnected web of universal consciousness.

These stones are more than conduits; they are reminders of a cosmic kinship that exists between humanity and the stars. Each crystal, each interaction, opens a doorway—a silent, unwavering call to those who wish to walk this path, a path that weaves through the mysteries of light and energy, of connection and transformation. In the Arcturian crystals lies a resonance that speaks to the heart of every seeker, a song of healing, balance, and profound unity with the fabric of the universe itself.

A resonance exists within Arcturian crystals that can only be felt, not described, a pulse that connects beyond boundaries and reaches into the core of one's being. This is the resonance of the Arcturian frequency, a singular vibration that bridges the physical and spiritual worlds, touching the human energetic field with a transformative power. Those who work with these crystals speak of a profound shift—a sense of being drawn into alignment with an energy that feels like an ancient, protective presence. But what does it mean to resonate with such a frequency, and how can it alter one's life?

For the practitioner, resonating with the Arcturian frequency through these crystals can bring subtle yet deep transformations. When held or placed in proximity to the body, Arcturian crystals act not merely as transmitters but as attuners, adjusting the vibrational field around and within, subtly raising one's energetic state. This resonance interacts with the practitioner's auric field, harmonizing it and strengthening its capacity to absorb and circulate energies of higher vibration. Many who work with these crystals describe an initial lightness that blossoms into clarity—a sensation of being in tune with a rhythm outside themselves, as if the crystal has attuned them to a state of calm, grounded equilibrium.

The Arcturian frequency is said to operate on wavelengths that benefit the human energy field, reaching into each layer and enhancing its inherent strengths. This frequency functions like a cosmic symphony that reorganizes chaotic energies into harmonious patterns, purging negativity and inviting higher states of consciousness. When one resonates with this frequency, it's as if a quiet yet potent wave sweeps through, removing the unseen knots and blockages that can cloud one's spirit. The result is a clearer path, an inner opening that enhances not only the flow of energy but a connection to higher guidance.

In this way, the resonance of Arcturian crystals acts as a foundation, establishing an energetic baseline from which transformation begins. The stones are known to amplify and reflect back the energy of the practitioner, a quality that allows them to serve as guides through emotional, physical, and spiritual transitions. By bringing one's energy field into resonance with the Arcturian frequency, the crystals work to create a gentle yet firm bridge between ordinary awareness and the subtle realms of higher consciousness. This effect is gradual and cumulative, developing over time as the practitioner attunes themselves to the crystal's energy, making it an enduring presence in their life.

Practitioners have found that this resonance has effects on all levels of the human experience. Physically, it brings a sense of relaxation, a calm in the body that promotes healing and helps the nervous system regulate itself, reducing stress and releasing tension held in the muscles and tissues. On an emotional level, the Arcturian frequency invites balance, quieting turbulent emotions and bringing a sense of centered peace that extends beyond individual practice sessions. Mentally, the resonance clears stagnant thoughts, dissolving the patterns of worry, fear, or overthinking that often dominate the mind. And spiritually, it opens doors—providing insights, flashes of intuition, and a heightened awareness that connects one to something far greater than oneself.

The process of working with this resonance requires both patience and openness, for the frequency operates on a level beyond the linear understanding of time. This is why those new to the practice are encouraged to begin by spending quiet moments in meditation with their Arcturian crystals, allowing the body and mind to absorb the frequency without expectation. Over time, practitioners find their own unique relationship to the energy, discovering how the crystals resonate with them individually, subtly shifting in response to the practitioner's needs and intentions. It is said that the stones reflect back the practitioner's spirit, amplifying what is needed in that moment and dissolving what is not.

With deeper practice, one begins to realize the full impact of resonating with the Arcturian frequency. This resonance does more than just harmonize; it creates a dynamic shield, a protective field around the body that reinforces one's natural boundaries. By attuning to the crystal's energy, one builds a layer of defense that guards against lower vibrations, shielding against energies that could disrupt one's inner state. This protective quality of the Arcturian frequency is not aggressive or forceful; it is simply an impenetrable calm that cannot be easily disturbed. For those who live or work in environments with dense or chaotic energy, this shield offers peace and security, a sanctuary in the midst of worldly demands.

The crystals become more than tools—they are allies in an ongoing process of inner strengthening and growth. With continued work, the resonance with the Arcturian frequency leads one toward personal transformation, guiding the spirit to reach beyond its former limitations and uncover layers of self-awareness and connection. Many practitioners find that with time, they are able to sense the crystal's energy without even holding it, as if the frequency has integrated with their own, becoming part of their being. In moments of stress or doubt, a quiet meditation on this resonance can rekindle the sense of harmony and inner calm, a reminder of the crystal's enduring presence.

Ultimately, resonating with the Arcturian frequency invites the practitioner to discover a depth within themselves, a part that feels timeless, centered, and connected to the universe in a way that defies language. It is a journey that begins with a simple crystal but unfolds into a lifetime of transformation, a path of quiet resilience and discovery that offers more than healing—it offers a vision of the self and the cosmos as interwoven, infinitely connected. And for those who answer the call of this frequency, the journey is one of constant evolution, a rhythm of light and energy that speaks to the innermost heart, always waiting to be heard.

Chapter 3
Preparing to Work with Crystals

In the realm of Arcturian crystals, the journey begins not with the crystals themselves but within the practitioner, for these stones respond to the energy and intentions of those who approach them. Just as one might clear and center before meditation, preparation is essential before engaging with these crystals. To open oneself to their energy, one must begin with a conscious alignment, creating a fertile ground for the crystal's frequency to harmonize with one's own. This preparation is an act of respect, a way to approach the Arcturian energy with clarity and purpose, ensuring that the practitioner is in a receptive state, attuned to the crystal's potential.

The practitioner's emotional and mental states play a crucial role in this preparatory phase, as each layer of the self must be clear and calm to fully receive the Arcturian frequency. This means entering into a practice with a sense of calm, a balanced mind, and a heart unburdened by residual negative emotions. To foster such an atmosphere, one may begin with a gentle process of breathwork. Slow, rhythmic breathing grounds the practitioner in the present moment, signaling to the body and mind that it is time to let go of daily concerns, stresses, and attachments that can obscure one's inner state. As the breath flows steadily, each inhalation invites calm and focus, each exhalation releases tension and clears the way for the energy to flow freely.

Intentions, too, must be consciously set, for these are the silent messages one sends to the crystals. Without clear intent, energy can be scattered, diluted in its effect. A few moments of reflection before working with the crystal allow the practitioner to align their goals, whether it be healing, protection, or simply a wish for clarity and connection. In focusing one's mind, the practitioner sets a vibration that the crystal can amplify, creating a direct channel between the human energy field and the crystalline resonance. Intentions should be simple, specific, and sincere, mirroring the clarity of Arcturian energy itself.

Some practitioners choose to hold their crystal lightly in hand as they form their intentions, feeling its cool, solid presence as a grounding force. Others prefer to place it nearby, allowing its frequency to subtly blend with their own. In either case, it is the connection between practitioner and crystal that matters most. This connection is forged not through words but through a quiet understanding, a willingness to enter into partnership with the energy. Arcturian crystals are said to respond to this openness, becoming more vibrant and active as they attune to the practitioner's energetic field. Those who hold the crystal may feel a tingling sensation or gentle warmth, signs that the crystal's frequency is beginning to interact with their own.

As the preparatory steps continue, the focus shifts inward, cultivating a state of openness. Visualization can play a powerful role here, helping to strengthen one's connection to the crystal. Some imagine themselves bathed in a soft, violet-blue light, the color often associated with Arcturian energy, flowing around and through them like a gentle river. This visualization creates a receptive energy field, enhancing the practitioner's ability to attune to the crystal's resonance. The visualization is less about seeing and more about feeling, sensing the presence of the Arcturian frequency merging with one's energy, a subtle yet profound connection that opens the doors to deeper work with the crystal.

Practitioners find that preparation allows them to access the crystal's energy with more ease and clarity, and the effects of this work are often experienced as calmness and grounded presence. Some even liken this preparatory state to a sacred ritual, a moment of quiet reverence for the forces they are about to engage with. This state of mind is essential, for it is only in a calm, focused state that the practitioner can fully receive the guidance and healing the crystal offers. Just as one would tune an instrument before a performance, preparation is a tuning of the mind, body, and spirit, aligning with the crystal's frequency for the most potent experience.

Emotional clarity also plays a vital role in preparation, for emotions are energies, and energies communicate. Negative emotions such as anger, fear, or frustration can cloud the interaction with the crystal, acting as barriers that block the resonance from flowing freely. To counter this, practitioners often take a few moments to release any emotional weight they may be carrying. Some choose to journal, releasing thoughts and feelings onto paper as a means of clearing the mind. Others may engage in gentle movement or stretching, allowing the body to release tension stored within muscles and joints. By the time one returns to the crystal, they are unburdened, free to engage fully and openly with the resonance that awaits them.

For those who wish to go further, additional preparation may include creating a quiet, intentional space. Many practitioners find that a dedicated area for working with Arcturian crystals enhances their experience. This space is typically free from distractions, a sanctuary where one can focus fully on their practice. Soft lighting, natural elements like plants or stones, and symbols that resonate with peace and balance create an environment conducive to the experience. Some may light incense or a candle, engaging the senses to deepen their focus and signal to the mind that this is a time of inward exploration and connection.

Through each preparatory step, practitioners honor the relationship they are about to build with the crystal, opening a pathway for the energy to flow freely. The ritual of preparation is not about rigid formality but a quiet respect, a way to approach the crystal with reverence, aligning with its energy before any exchange takes place. In this state, the practitioner is like a clear vessel, open to receive and harmonize with the crystal's gifts.

Once the inner clarity is achieved, and intentions are set, a deeper layer of preparation awaits those who wish to harmonize fully with Arcturian crystals. This layer engages the practitioner's energy on a cellular level, a process of self-adjustment that invites the crystal's frequency to merge more profoundly with one's own. These rituals, though simple in practice, create an energy alignment that enhances one's connection to the Arcturian resonance, guiding the practitioner into a state of harmony before beginning their work with the crystal.

One of the most effective preparatory practices is energy self-adjustment through breathing techniques. The breath serves as the bridge between body and spirit, a silent rhythm that weaves together mind and energy. With a calm and steady breath, one can bring the nervous system into a balanced state, relaxing muscles and preparing the mind for connection. A common technique is the "three-phase breath," where practitioners inhale slowly, allowing the air to fill their lower abdomen, then the chest, and finally, up to the collarbones, pausing briefly before exhaling in the reverse order. This three-part breath mirrors the expansion and contraction of universal energy, centering the practitioner in a state of calm readiness.

In addition to breathing, concentration techniques play a critical role in self-adjustment. Arcturian energy, being subtle and layered, requires a focused mind to fully engage with its frequency. For this reason, many practitioners spend a few moments each day honing their concentration through single-pointed focus exercises. One approach is to concentrate on a small object or point of light, such as the tip of a candle flame or the surface of the crystal itself. This focus clears the mind of distractions, allowing one to become present and attuned to the subtleties of energy. Through this practice, the practitioner's awareness becomes as steady as the crystal's resonance, preparing the mind to receive the Arcturian energy without obstruction.

Beyond concentration, mentalization exercises enhance the practitioner's ability to connect with the crystal on a vibrational level. Mentalization is a form of visualization with intention, where one sees the energy within the mind's eye as though it were a tangible field surrounding the body. In this exercise, practitioners visualize themselves encased in a light-filled sphere, a protective aura that aligns with the Arcturian energy. They see the light grow brighter and more radiant, blending with the crystal's frequency and forming a harmonious connection. This mentalization creates a symbolic bridge between the practitioner and the crystal, a preparation of the inner world to match the outer resonance, allowing the Arcturian energy to flow more freely.

Self-adjustment practices continue with the incorporation of sensory alignment, where the practitioner connects to the crystal through touch, sound, or even scent. Each of these elements engages the senses, helping the body and mind remember the state of calmness and receptivity. Holding the crystal gently, one might close their eyes and let their fingertips trace its contours, sensing the texture and weight, becoming familiar with the stone as though meeting an old friend. By focusing on touch, the practitioner grounds themselves, bringing their awareness back to the present moment. Others may use sound, chanting a simple hum or mantra, allowing the vibrations of the voice to blend with the crystal's energy, setting an auditory tone that resonates with the Arcturian frequency.

Another powerful step in preparing to work with Arcturian crystals is setting an energetic anchor. This is an internal symbol or feeling that the practitioner associates with balance and harmony, an anchor they can return to throughout their practice. This anchor might be a word, like "peace" or "clarity," or a physical sensation, such as the warmth of the breath. By focusing on this anchor, the practitioner creates a steady point of reference, a reminder that the connection with the Arcturian crystal is not just external but a shared frequency they carry within themselves. This anchor becomes a tether to the crystal's resonance, helping the practitioner remain attuned even when life's stresses and distractions arise.

Some practitioners choose to create a ceremonial space around them, setting aside a specific area where they can engage with the crystal's energy undisturbed. In this space, certain objects may hold symbolic value—incense to cleanse, soft lighting to calm, or a small altar where the crystal rests between sessions. Creating a dedicated space strengthens the connection to the Arcturian energy, allowing the practitioner to enter a state of deep receptivity. Each item becomes part of the ritual, reinforcing the intention to harmonize with the crystal's frequency, to meet it with respect and clarity.

In preparing oneself and the environment, the practitioner enters a sacred moment, a space in time set apart to fully engage with the energy of the Arcturian crystal. And though the steps may seem simple, each action serves a purpose, guiding the practitioner deeper into resonance with the crystal's frequency. This preparation process is not rigid but fluid, allowing each individual to discover the practices that resonate most deeply with them, adjusting as they become more attuned to the crystal's energy.

With each preparation ritual, the practitioner aligns more closely with the Arcturian frequency, creating a foundation for meaningful interaction with the crystal. These practices invite a profound respect for the energy, an understanding that this connection is a living exchange, an ebb and flow that brings practitioner and crystal into perfect harmony. And so, the process of preparation becomes an act of devotion, a gesture of alignment and openness that bridges the ordinary and the extraordinary, guiding one to experience the crystal's energy not as an external force, but as a part of their own unfolding journey.

Chapter 4
Purifying and Activating Crystals

The preparation to work with Arcturian crystals begins with reverence, but the journey unfolds further with a vital step: purification and activation. Crystals, like sponges, absorb energies from the spaces they occupy, as well as from those who handle them. To work with Arcturian crystals in their purest form, practitioners must first cleanse them, releasing any accumulated energy that could disrupt the crystal's innate resonance. Purification is a ritual of renewal, a way to bring the crystal back to its original, untouched state, allowing it to function as a clear conduit for the Arcturian frequency.

Smudging, one of the most ancient and effective purification methods, is commonly used to cleanse crystals. With the smoke from sacred herbs such as sage, cedar, or palo santo, the practitioner envelopes the crystal, allowing the smoke to drift around and through it, carrying away any stagnant or discordant energies. The aroma of these herbs is said to be cleansing, grounding, and protective, acting as a bridge between the earthly and spiritual realms. As the smoke coils around the crystal, practitioners may visualize any lingering energies dissolving, dispersing into the air, leaving the crystal vibrant and renewed.

Another revered technique is moonlight exposure. The soft, silver glow of the moon, particularly during its full phase, bathes the crystal in a light that revitalizes its energy without overpowering it. By placing the crystal under the open sky, practitioners allow the crystal to absorb the moon's subtle frequencies, a process that aligns the stone with the cyclical rhythms of nature. The moon's energy is thought to be both feminine and nurturing, a gentle influence that amplifies the Arcturian crystal's connection to the ethereal. Practitioners often leave their crystals out overnight, trusting that by dawn, the crystal will have absorbed the renewing essence of the moonlight, purged of any unwanted vibrations.

Some practitioners choose to purify their crystals by immersing them in salt, a mineral known for its powerful cleansing properties. Sea salt, in particular, is believed to draw out impurities, neutralizing any unaligned energies within the crystal. To protect the stone's surface, practitioners may place the crystal in a small cloth bag before submerging it in a bowl of salt, ensuring that it is enveloped but unharmed. Salt purification is especially useful for crystals that may have absorbed dense or challenging energies, for it returns the crystal to its elemental purity, grounded and clear.

With purification complete, the next step is activation—a practice that invites the crystal to awaken and align with the practitioner's specific purpose. Activation is not simply about infusing the crystal with intention; it is an energetic "awakening," a way of bringing the stone's natural powers to the surface. This process, while gentle, is transformative, for it marks the beginning of a unique connection between the crystal and its holder. As the crystal becomes attuned, it develops a resonance that reflects both the Arcturian frequency and the practitioner's purpose, creating a bond that enhances the energy exchange.

One activation method is intention setting, a quiet, focused moment where the practitioner holds the crystal close, speaking or mentally transmitting their purpose to it. With closed eyes, one might focus on the qualities they wish to imbue—healing, protection, insight, or balance. It is a time of quiet communication, where the practitioner and crystal harmonize, each attuning to the other. This step is often accompanied by visualization, where the practitioner imagines a radiant light filling the crystal, a glow that symbolizes the energy of their intention. This light may take on a color or a shape that represents the desired qualities, infusing the crystal with a focused and active purpose.

Some practitioners activate their crystals by placing them on natural surfaces, like earth or stone, allowing the crystal to reestablish its connection to the Earth. This grounding technique reinforces the crystal's bond with its natural origins, while also harmonizing it with the planetary energies that support its work. By placing the crystal on bare earth, the practitioner invites it to draw strength from the ground itself, creating a stable foundation for the frequencies it will carry. This grounding serves as a powerful activation, linking the Arcturian resonance with the earthbound frequencies of the practitioner's environment.

It is also common for practitioners to sing or chant softly while activating their crystals, using their voice as a vibrational tool to bring the crystal into resonance with the Arcturian frequency. The voice carries intention through sound, a vibration that reaches the crystal's structure and calls forth its latent energy. The chant may be a personal mantra or an intuitive sound, a vibration felt deeply in the practitioner's chest or heart. Through the resonance of their own voice, the practitioner aligns their energy with the crystal's, creating an activation that is unique, a moment where the crystal and its holder become partners in purpose.

Each method of purification and activation contributes to a foundation of mutual respect between the crystal and its practitioner. Through the care of these rituals, the practitioner acknowledges the crystal as an ally in their spiritual journey, a partner in healing, protection, and guidance. These actions invite the Arcturian frequency into a clear, unencumbered space, ensuring that the energy flows freely, unimpeded by past interactions or environmental residues.

With each purification, the crystal's energy is renewed, and with each activation, it awakens a little more to the practitioner's purpose. The crystal becomes a vessel for intentions, a beacon of resonance, a point of connection to the vast Arcturian energies that permeate all things. And in turn, the practitioner becomes a part of this flow, a conduit through which the Arcturian frequency can unfold its mysteries, touching every aspect of life with its quiet, profound presence. Through these acts of renewal and alignment, the crystal becomes a living part of the practitioner's path, a partner in the dance of light, purpose, and endless discovery.

Once the foundation of purification and activation is established, the journey into refining these practices continues, inviting a deeper and more personalized resonance with each crystal. The use of mantras and visualizations adds yet another layer of intention, a vibrational link that aligns the crystal with the Arcturian frequency in an intimate and powerful way. Through these methods, the practitioner transforms the crystal into a finely tuned vessel for Arcturian energy, ensuring that its purpose is not only set but harmonized with the higher dimensions.

Mantras serve as conduits of energy, their vibrations creating subtle yet powerful alignments within the crystal's structure. Each syllable carries an intention, a specific resonance that the crystal absorbs and amplifies. Practitioners often begin by selecting a mantra that reflects their goal—words or sounds that resonate with healing, protection, or clarity. As they chant, they hold the crystal in their hand or place it before them, visualizing each soundwave entering the stone. Over time, the crystal adopts the mantra's frequency, becoming a beacon of the intended energy, a silent partner that echoes the vibrations set forth.

While chanting, the practitioner might envision threads of light connecting them with the crystal. This light, flowing from their heart or third eye, symbolizes the unity between human energy and the crystal's inherent resonance. Each word, each pulse of sound, serves as a rhythm that binds practitioner and crystal, creating a synergy that awakens the crystal's potential. As they focus on this, practitioners often find themselves becoming attuned to the subtle shifts within the crystal, sensing its energy strengthen and radiate outward, absorbing the intention with each repetition.

Visualization, another powerful tool in the activation process, allows the practitioner to set a vivid energetic signature within the crystal. Here, they imagine the crystal glowing with colors that represent the desired qualities—healing might be a soft green, protection a deep blue, clarity a radiant white. This color-filled energy is imagined infusing the crystal, illuminating it from within. The practitioner visualizes this light expanding and pulsating, growing stronger with each breath, filling the crystal and surrounding it with a vibrant aura that resonates with the Arcturian frequency.

For some, this visualization may include images of Arcturian landscapes or symbols that resonate with cosmic energies—stars, distant galaxies, or abstract forms that evoke a sense of the Arcturian realm. These images serve as touchpoints, creating a bridge between the earthly and the cosmic, connecting the practitioner to the crystal in a way that transcends physical form. By envisioning the crystal as part of a greater cosmic landscape, they imbue it with a sense of purpose that aligns with the vastness and peace of Arcturian energies.

In addition to these techniques, many practitioners employ a final step: setting the crystal's purpose with a focused intention, a silent affirmation of the specific role the crystal will play. This could be a simple mental directive, such as "Be a source of healing" or "Provide protection and clarity." This intention serves as the cornerstone of activation, giving the crystal a role within the practitioner's energy field. By establishing this purpose, the crystal becomes a conscious ally, an active participant in the journey of healing and spiritual discovery.

There is a practice known as "energy imprinting," where the practitioner places the crystal against their third eye or heart chakra, allowing a natural exchange of energy to flow between them. Here, the practitioner visualizes the crystal absorbing their energy signature, their individual resonance merging with the crystal's. This step is gentle yet profound, a final act of attunement that aligns the crystal not only with the Arcturian frequency but with the unique vibration of the practitioner. The result is a crystal that is not only powerful in its own right but uniquely attuned to its holder, a true companion in the work of energy and transformation.

Through each ritual of purification and activation, the practitioner refines the crystal, strengthening its ability to resonate with the Arcturian energy. With each mantra, each visualization, each intention, the crystal becomes a clearer, more focused tool, a vessel that carries both the Arcturian frequency and the practitioner's unique purpose. These rituals serve not only to prepare the crystal but to deepen the practitioner's bond with it, inviting them into a partnership that holds the potential for healing, protection, and a continuous unfolding of spiritual insight.

In this way, the crystal becomes more than a stone; it is an extension of the practitioner's own energy, a mirror of their intentions, a channel for the wisdom of the Arcturian realm. And in each moment of work, this connection grows, weaving practitioner and crystal together in the silent dance of resonance and purpose, a journey guided by light and intention.

Chapter 5
Healing Energy and Properties

To understand the true depth of Arcturian crystals, one must step into the mystery of their healing properties. Within these stones lies an energy that moves with purpose and precision, a frequency designed not merely to resonate but to heal, aligning the physical, emotional, and spiritual layers of being. This healing energy is unique, distinct from other forms of crystal healing, as it emanates from a frequency that taps into the Arcturian realm—a cosmic force that operates beyond the ordinary layers of energy known to the earthly realm.

Those who work with Arcturian crystals for healing often describe a sensation that reaches deeper than traditional stones. The energy does not flood or overpower but rather seeps gently, reaching into the roots of imbalance with a calm, focused presence. These stones carry a frequency that is both grounding and elevating, and the dual nature of their energy allows them to harmonize with various levels of the self. The practitioner feels the energy as a soft pulse or a quiet hum that reverberates through the body, touching points of tension, illness, or misalignment, and offering a gentle realignment that fosters healing at the deepest level.

The healing energy of Arcturian crystals seems to respond intuitively to the body's needs. When held or placed upon areas of physical discomfort, their frequency interacts with the natural rhythms of the body, working to dissolve blockages and restore energetic flow. Many practitioners find that their physical pain softens under the influence of these crystals, as though the stones know precisely where the energy is needed most. The Arcturian resonance flows into the body's meridians, those hidden rivers of energy that govern wellness and vitality, cleansing and realigning them to allow the life force to move freely once more.

On an emotional level, the crystals bring healing that resonates through the heart and mind, quieting turmoil, easing anxieties, and providing a calm that feels almost unearthly. When one holds an Arcturian crystal with the intention of emotional healing, the stone acts as a balm, drawing out emotional blockages and helping to release pent-up feelings with grace and ease. It is as though the crystal listens, absorbing the burdens of the heart and gently guiding them into release, helping the practitioner to find balance and clarity. For those who suffer from persistent worries or deep-seated fears, the crystal's frequency offers a doorway into peace, lifting the emotional weight and allowing the spirit to breathe freely.

The Arcturian frequency also has a unique effect on the mental body, helping to clear away fogginess and mental clutter. When one sits in meditation with an Arcturian crystal, particularly one set with the intention of clarity or focus, the mind often becomes clearer, more ordered. This crystal energy gently dissolves distracting thoughts and worries, allowing the mind to settle into a calm, receptive state. Practitioners report feeling as though a weight has lifted from their thoughts, as though the crystal sweeps away layers of confusion, leaving behind a sense of mental clarity and peace. This quality makes Arcturian crystals a valuable tool for those seeking insight, focus, or an enhanced ability to meditate deeply.

Beyond physical and emotional healing, Arcturian crystals possess a capacity for spiritual restoration that resonates within the soul. These stones are like keys, unlocking pathways to higher awareness and self-discovery. As one works with them, the crystals invite the practitioner to access realms of spiritual insight and healing, to venture beyond the limitations of ordinary consciousness into spaces of clarity and understanding. This form of healing is subtle, often experienced as a gradual opening rather than a sudden revelation. The crystals' energy brings the practitioner closer to the Arcturian frequency, guiding them to an awareness that transcends the self, a state where inner wounds begin to soften in the presence of a universal light.

Those who incorporate these stones into their spiritual practices often find that the healing energy seeps into every layer of their being, creating a resonance that lasts long after the crystal is set down. It is as if the energy, once absorbed, lingers within the practitioner, continuing to align and uplift long after the initial interaction. The resonance of Arcturian crystals nurtures an ongoing relationship with the energies of healing and growth, a connection that transforms each aspect of life. For many, this is the beginning of a personal journey into deeper levels of self-awareness, a path illuminated by the subtle yet profound light that these crystals carry.

Arcturian crystals have also been known to amplify the body's natural healing processes, harmonizing with the cells themselves to encourage regeneration and vitality. This amplification is not forceful but supportive, a gentle urging of the body's innate ability to heal. When placed upon areas of physical need, the crystal's frequency merges with the cellular structure, creating an environment conducive to recovery and strength. Those who work with the crystals for physical healing often feel a warmth or tingling, a sensation that signals the flow of energy as it supports the body's own wisdom and resilience.

In each use, the practitioner discovers that Arcturian crystals are more than just healing tools; they are partners, allies in the journey toward wholeness. Their frequency is patient, their energy enduring, always ready to meet the needs of the moment with a gentle yet profound embrace. This makes them uniquely suited to sustained healing practices, where their effects grow over time, deepening with each interaction. As they continue to work with these stones, practitioners find that their connection to the Arcturian frequency grows stronger, their energy field more resilient, their mind clearer, and their heart more open.

The healing properties of Arcturian crystals are as boundless as the energy from which they originate, a force that reaches into the hidden realms of existence, offering transformation not only in the present moment but in every moment thereafter. To hold one is to experience this journey, to step into the flow of a cosmic frequency that heals, restores, and guides the spirit, bringing it ever closer to the light of the stars.

As the healing journey with Arcturian crystals deepens, the practitioner discovers the profound ways in which these stones can be directed toward specific healing purposes. Each Arcturian crystal acts as a focused channel, able to address particular needs with precision and purpose. In the process, the practitioner not only unlocks the crystal's potential but also becomes more attuned to the intricacies of their own energy field, learning to guide the crystal's power toward areas of greatest need. This conscious direction of energy transforms the crystal from a passive object to an active tool, a partner in the journey of physical, emotional, and spiritual restoration.

For physical healing, Arcturian crystals can be directed to focus on individual areas of the body that require support. Practitioners often begin by identifying areas of pain or imbalance, gently holding the crystal to that place and inviting the energy to flow into it. The Arcturian frequency interacts with the body's natural healing processes, encouraging alignment and balance in areas where energy may have become stagnant. As the crystal is held to the site, its resonance merges with the body's energy, creating a flow that feels almost like a gentle warmth or soft pulse. This interaction brings life back into tired cells, subtly urging the physical tissues to return to harmony.

For those experiencing muscular tension or discomfort, placing the crystal along meridian points or energy centers (chakras) can amplify its effect. The energy of the crystal moves through these channels, reaching deeper into the body's structure to relieve tightness and ease tension. This technique works well for both acute pain and chronic conditions, as the Arcturian energy not only targets the physical discomfort but also addresses underlying emotional and energetic blockages that may contribute to the pain. The crystal becomes a focused point of healing, gently restoring balance to areas that have long held tension or trauma.

Arcturian crystals are equally powerful in addressing emotional healing. Here, they act almost like a compassionate presence, easing wounds that lie hidden within the heart and mind. When held with the intent of emotional support, the crystal's energy brings a calm, reassuring resonance, one that invites the practitioner to release burdens, sadness, or fears that may be weighing on their spirit. Some hold the crystal close to the heart, allowing its frequency to merge with the emotional body, while visualizing their emotional pain flowing into the crystal, where it can be transformed and released.

This process can bring about a profound sense of relief, as if the crystal absorbs the weight of unspoken sorrows, replacing them with a feeling of lightness and inner peace. Practitioners who work with Arcturian crystals over time often find that their emotional state becomes more stable, as though each interaction gradually clears away layers of unresolved feelings, replacing them with clarity and openness. It is as if the crystal's energy envelops the practitioner, creating a sanctuary of healing, a safe space in which the heart can find balance and renewal.

In addition to emotional and physical healing, Arcturian crystals offer an unparalleled support in mental clarity and focus. When directed toward the mind, the crystal's energy clears away distractions, dissolving worry, doubt, or mental clutter that may obscure the practitioner's focus. During meditation or moments of quiet reflection, practitioners place the crystal upon their third eye, inviting its frequency to flow directly into the mind. This placement allows the energy to interact with the thought processes, clarifying and calming the mind, as though clearing a path through dense fog.

With the third eye as the focal point, the crystal's energy sharpens intuition, aiding in moments where insight is needed, or decisions are difficult. Practitioners describe feeling as though their thoughts align with greater ease, each one flowing naturally into the next without interruption. It is a sense of mental flow, where clarity replaces confusion, allowing for enhanced focus and a deeper connection to inner wisdom. This mental healing is invaluable not only in spiritual practices but in daily life, providing the practitioner with a tool for grounding their thoughts and returning to their natural state of balance.

Arcturian crystals can also be directed toward spiritual healing, where their energy resonates within the layers of the soul, guiding the practitioner toward self-discovery and expanded consciousness. Here, the crystal's purpose goes beyond addressing specific issues, reaching instead into the essence of the practitioner's being. Through meditative practices, practitioners direct the crystal's energy into areas of their spiritual life that require healing or insight. In this way, the crystal's frequency acts as a light, illuminating hidden aspects of the self and allowing deeper truths to emerge.

During these sessions, practitioners often feel a deepening of their spiritual connection, as if the crystal has opened a doorway to realms of understanding that were previously inaccessible. The energy resonates with the higher self, helping to integrate these insights in a way that feels grounded and nurturing. This practice can be particularly powerful for those seeking a deeper sense of purpose or alignment, as the crystal offers a pathway toward self-realization, a journey into the heart of one's true nature.

The effects of Arcturian crystals are cumulative, growing with each interaction, as the practitioner's relationship with the crystal deepens. Over time, the body and mind become more receptive to the crystal's energy, allowing for a more fluid exchange that brings about lasting change. Practitioners often describe feeling a sense of wholeness as they continue this work, an alignment that extends beyond the physical body and resonates with the soul itself. This is the essence of healing with Arcturian crystals—a journey that goes beyond treating symptoms, inviting the practitioner to explore the full spectrum of self, from the physical to the spiritual, guided by a frequency as ancient as the stars.

Through specific healing sessions, each practitioner learns to direct the energy of these crystals to where it is most needed, to use them as partners in transformation, as mirrors of inner wholeness. And so, these crystals become more than simple tools; they are touchstones of healing, carrying the light of the Arcturian realm into the depths of human experience, harmonizing, aligning, and restoring the practitioner to their truest, most balanced self.

Chapter 6
Connection with the Frequency

The journey of working with Arcturian crystals is not merely one of utilizing energy but of forming a deep, conscious connection with the Arcturian frequency. This energy flows beyond the limitations of the physical realm, carrying with it a wisdom that transcends the ordinary senses, reaching into the essence of spiritual understanding. Developing a bond with this frequency is an unfolding process, one that requires attunement, patience, and a readiness to open oneself to the unseen dimensions of energy that these crystals channel.

For practitioners, the first step toward establishing this connection begins with the practice of tuning into the subtle vibrations that radiate from the crystal. Arcturian crystals hold a frequency that is often experienced as a gentle hum or soft pulsation, something that can be felt through focused attention. Many begin by holding the crystal lightly, feeling its cool, smooth surface, and closing their eyes to tune into the sensations it emits. This tuning-in process invites the practitioner to slow down, breathe deeply, and allow the mind to quiet, creating a stillness where the Arcturian frequency can be perceived in its true form.

The breath is a powerful ally in this practice, for it not only grounds the practitioner but also creates a rhythm that aligns with the crystal's energy. As the practitioner breathes slowly and deeply, they allow the breath to draw the frequency into their body, imagining it flowing from the crystal and merging with their own energy field. With each inhalation, they bring the crystal's essence closer, feeling the energy radiate from their heart center or third eye, two energetic points often associated with higher awareness. This rhythm of breath and intention creates a bridge, allowing the Arcturian frequency to permeate the practitioner's energy field.

An integral part of building this connection is learning to sense the crystal's response to the practitioner's energy. When attuned to the crystal's frequency, many feel a reciprocal exchange, as though the crystal itself is responding, aligning its energy with the practitioner's. This experience is subtle, often felt as a gentle warmth, a tingling in the hands, or even a slight sensation of lightness. These responses signal the beginning of a relationship—a dialogue of energies that will continue to evolve, deepening the bond between practitioner and crystal with each session.

To deepen this bond, practitioners may engage in a visualization practice, one that brings them closer to the essence of the Arcturian realm. In this exercise, they imagine themselves surrounded by a soft, violet-blue light, a hue often associated with the Arcturian frequency. This light flows around them, infusing their energy field with a feeling of calm, balance, and subtle expansion. As the light surrounds them, they visualize the crystal in their hand glowing in harmony, its own radiance merging with the aura around them. This shared light creates a sense of unity, as though the crystal and practitioner are one, resonating within the same frequency, harmonizing both their energies.

As this practice unfolds, a sensitivity to the crystal's energy grows, a recognition of the subtle ways the Arcturian frequency influences thoughts, feelings, and even perceptions. Practitioners may find that, over time, their awareness of this energy becomes more natural, as though the frequency has become part of their daily rhythm. This presence is not overwhelming but a gentle reminder of the connection that reaches beyond the visible world, a thread that links them to the Arcturian wisdom. Some describe this as a quiet knowing, an intuitive awareness that gently guides them through moments of decision or reflection, providing a sense of clarity and calm.

For those seeking a deeper resonance, incorporating a meditation practice with the crystal further enhances the bond. The crystal can be placed before the practitioner during meditation, or held in the hands, while they allow their mind to quiet, focusing entirely on the energy of the crystal. As they settle into stillness, they envision themselves journeying into the Arcturian frequency, a space of expansive light and peace, where insights arise naturally and the distractions of the ordinary world fade. Here, the crystal serves as a guide, an anchor that grounds the practitioner in the Arcturian frequency, while also opening the door to spiritual realms that lie beyond ordinary perception.

The conscious connection with the Arcturian frequency invites more than an energetic exchange; it is an invitation to discover a new layer of self-awareness. By tuning in, practitioners often find themselves more attuned to their own needs, rhythms, and states of mind. This frequency acts like a mirror, reflecting back not only the energy of the Arcturian realm but also aspects of the practitioner's inner world that may have remained unseen. It becomes a tool for self-reflection, a quiet companion that gently brings to light areas of growth, healing, and spiritual development.

Through regular connection practices, the practitioner also begins to sense a strengthening in their own energy field. This connection with the Arcturian frequency creates a protective layer, a subtle shield that fortifies their aura against disruptive or negative energies. This shielding effect is not rigid or forceful; it feels more like a soft resonance that naturally repels any energy that does not align with the practitioner's highest good. As the connection with the frequency grows, so does this natural protection, an enduring presence that remains with the practitioner even outside of dedicated practice sessions.

Over time, this connection becomes less of an exercise and more of an instinctive part of the practitioner's life. The crystal's energy becomes a familiar presence, like a quiet current flowing alongside them, subtly influencing their thoughts, emotions, and interactions. This frequency is no longer an external force but a part of the practitioner's inner landscape, a resonance that can be drawn upon in moments of challenge or uncertainty, providing a constant reminder of the Arcturian wisdom and light.

Through these practices, the connection with the Arcturian frequency becomes an unfolding path, one that brings balance, insight, and a gentle strength that flows into every area of life. The crystal becomes a doorway, a companion on this path, guiding the practitioner deeper into realms of energy and self-awareness, a journey where the frequency of light and wisdom becomes a permanent part of the practitioner's own inner landscape.

As the connection with the Arcturian frequency deepens, practitioners are invited to explore rituals that further enhance their bond with this energy. These rituals serve as doorways into a more profound experience with the Arcturian resonance, drawing practitioners into a heightened state of awareness that amplifies the crystal's power and allows for transformative insight. Engaging in these rituals with dedication and presence, practitioners find that the Arcturian frequency not only surrounds them but begins to flow through them, becoming a part of their very being.

One of the most effective practices for establishing a strong connection is through meditative postures that align the body with the energy of the crystal. Sitting in a comfortable posture, often cross-legged with a straight spine, the practitioner holds the crystal gently at heart level or places it upon their lap. This posture creates an open channel through which the energy can flow unobstructed, allowing the Arcturian frequency to rise from the crystal into the practitioner's energetic field. With closed eyes, the practitioner takes slow, intentional breaths, each inhalation drawing the crystal's energy inward, each exhalation releasing any tension or resistance.

This breathwork is not merely a physical practice but an energetic tuning that harmonizes the body's rhythm with the crystal's frequency. Practitioners often find that as they breathe in this way, the boundaries between themselves and the crystal begin to dissolve. The Arcturian frequency fills them, seeping into the spaces between thoughts, aligning the mind and heart with the clarity of cosmic energy. In this state, the crystal's energy moves beyond the physical and into the spiritual, weaving a thread of light that connects the practitioner's consciousness with the higher dimensions of the Arcturian realm.

Guided breathing can further enhance this connection, drawing the practitioner deeper into resonance with the crystal. For this practice, one might begin with a pattern of four counts in, holding for four counts, then exhaling for four, a rhythm that balances both mind and energy. As they breathe, the practitioner imagines the crystal's energy entering through the crown of the head, flowing down the spine and pooling at the heart, a center of harmony and balance. Here, the energy lingers, radiating outward, filling the practitioner's aura with the essence of the Arcturian frequency. This guided breath creates a sense of spaciousness, a moment where the self feels immersed within a field of light, connected to the crystal's energy and beyond, to the cosmos itself.

For those seeking a deeper spiritual immersion, chanting or vocal toning can be integrated into the ritual, using the power of sound to enhance the connection. The vibrations of the voice resonate through the body, creating a channel for the frequency to flow even more freely. Practitioners often chant softly, allowing the sound to emerge naturally, a tone or syllable that feels intuitive. The vibrations amplify the crystal's energy, each tone resonating with the subtle frequencies held within the stone. This practice brings a palpable sense of the Arcturian energy filling the space, as though each note summons the crystal's wisdom into the physical realm, an audible connection that reaches both inward and outward.

Visualization also plays a powerful role in strengthening this connection, as the mind's focus is directed toward the crystal's energy. Practitioners often imagine themselves standing within a circle of light, surrounded by stars, galaxies, or ethereal forms that represent the vastness of the Arcturian dimension. In this visualization, the crystal is imagined as a radiant center within this cosmic landscape, its light shining outward, merging with the practitioner's own energy. The visualization fosters a sense of unity, a recognition that the energy of the Arcturian crystal is not separate but part of a greater flow, a continuous thread that ties the practitioner to realms of light and wisdom.

Through these rituals, practitioners begin to experience the Arcturian frequency as more than an external energy; it becomes an element of their inner world. As the crystal's resonance merges with the practitioner's energy field, a transformation occurs. The frequency aligns with their spiritual centers, particularly the heart and third eye, enhancing intuition, compassion, and clarity. Over time, this connection solidifies, becoming a natural part of the practitioner's life, a silent presence that guides their actions, thoughts, and emotions with a wisdom that feels both ancient and new.

As the connection with the frequency grows, practitioners may find themselves more sensitive to the energies around them, experiencing heightened intuition and an awareness that feels almost perceptive. This sensitivity is not overwhelming but rather serves as a tool, a way to perceive the world with a clarity and depth that extends beyond the ordinary. The Arcturian frequency becomes a guide, a quiet voice that whispers insights and reveals truths that might otherwise go unnoticed, a sense of knowing that feels both instinctual and profound.

In the final stages of this ritual practice, practitioners are encouraged to take a moment of gratitude, honoring the crystal for its role in bridging this connection. By holding the crystal close, they acknowledge its partnership, a vessel of cosmic light that has opened doors to self-discovery and spiritual connection. This gratitude completes the ritual, sealing the energy exchange, reinforcing the connection with the Arcturian realm, and strengthening the crystal's bond with the practitioner's heart.

These practices for connecting with the Arcturian frequency are not bound by ritual but are meant to flow, adapting as the practitioner deepens their relationship with the energy.

Each session opens new pathways, inviting a fresh understanding of self and spirit, of the crystal's resonance and the endless potential held within the Arcturian light. Through each meditation, chant, or visualization, the crystal becomes a gateway, leading the practitioner ever closer to the wisdom and harmony of the cosmic energy that flows through all things.

Chapter 7
Energy Shield

In the delicate and unseen layers of energy surrounding each of us, there is a natural vulnerability to external influences. Some energies, like the warmth of shared joy or the peace of a sacred space, nourish the soul. Others, however, can drain or unsettle, affecting one's emotional, physical, and spiritual balance. Arcturian crystals offer a unique way to create an energetic shield, a form of protection that resonates with the Arcturian frequency, enveloping the practitioner in a field of light that guards against disruptive or negative forces. This shielding process is not only a practice of fortification but a step toward cultivating inner resilience, creating a space in which the soul can thrive without interference.

To begin building an energy shield with an Arcturian crystal, the practitioner holds the stone close, often at the heart or in both hands, as they center their intention on protection. This initial step involves setting a clear purpose for the crystal's energy: to shield, to guard, to protect. The practitioner envisions the crystal's frequency expanding outward, creating a sphere of light that surrounds their entire being. This visualization becomes a living shield, one that not only surrounds the body but also interweaves with the layers of the practitioner's aura, strengthening it from within.

Breath becomes an essential tool in activating and stabilizing this protective shield. Practitioners may start with deep, rhythmic breathing, each inhalation drawing in strength, each exhalation releasing any tension or lingering fears. With each breath, they envision the crystal's light growing, radiating outward in soft waves that form a protective cocoon around the body. This light feels tangible, almost like a gentle embrace that reassures the spirit, providing a calm space within which the practitioner can feel fully grounded and safe.

One of the most effective methods for fortifying this shield is to incorporate a visualization of colors, using shades that resonate with the Arcturian frequency, often violet or indigo, colors that carry a high vibration of peace and protection. The practitioner visualizes this color pulsing around them, flowing from the crystal as though the stone itself is alive, working to protect and uplift. The violet hue, rich and deep, feels like an impenetrable layer, allowing only positivity to enter and leaving negativity outside the shield's boundary. This color frequency blends with the Arcturian energy, creating a powerful vibration that both grounds and elevates, guarding the spirit from energies that would unsettle or distract.

The crystal's shield not only blocks external energies but also reinforces the practitioner's internal strength, creating a layer of resilience that endures even when the crystal is not physically present. Through regular practice, the crystal's shielding effect integrates with the practitioner's natural aura, so that, over time, the shield becomes an instinctive part of their energy field, available whenever protection is needed. It is a layer of peace that the practitioner carries within, a reminder of their ability to stay centered and safe amidst the world's shifting energies.

In moments of heightened vulnerability, such as crowded environments or emotionally intense situations, practitioners can strengthen the shield by focusing on the crystal and invoking its protective energy. By holding the crystal or visualizing it in hand, they mentally call forth its frequency, imagining the light thickening around them, solidifying into a protective barrier that cannot be breached. This mental reinforcement can be done discreetly, even in the midst of daily life, as a quiet, steadying ritual that invites the Arcturian energy to envelop and protect the practitioner, providing a refuge of calm and clarity.

Practitioners often find that over time, the crystal's shield provides not only protection but a sense of inner peace, a harmony that repels chaotic or draining influences simply by its presence. This protective layer allows the practitioner to move through life with an ease and confidence that feels new, a silent strength that upholds their own energy without depletion. The Arcturian frequency works quietly, guiding them to engage only with energies that align with their highest self, filtering out anything that may disturb or drain.

Working with this shield of Arcturian energy teaches the practitioner a form of spiritual resilience, a knowing that they are equipped to navigate both the seen and unseen realms without fear. The crystal's light serves as a constant, silent protector, a reminder of the cosmic guardianship that Arcturian energy provides. As the practitioner strengthens their relationship with the crystal, they find that this shield becomes more responsive, adapting to different environments, adjusting itself to provide exactly the protection needed for each moment.

In creating this energy shield, practitioners learn to live with a sense of spiritual autonomy, a quiet confidence that their energy is safe and their path secure. The Arcturian crystal stands as a steadfast partner in this practice, a stone that holds within it the vastness of the stars, guiding the practitioner to become a guardian of their own energy, moving through the world with clarity, peace, and a strength that resonates from within.

As the practice of energy shielding with Arcturian crystals deepens, practitioners are invited to refine and strengthen this protective barrier, customizing the shield to adapt to various situations and specific energetic needs. This process transforms the crystal's shield from a static layer into a dynamic field, one that responds to the unique circumstances of each moment. The practice becomes an art of tuning the shield's frequency, allowing it to harmonize seamlessly with the environment while filtering out unwanted energies.

One of the most profound ways to customize the shield is by directing the crystal's energy into layers, creating a multi-dimensional barrier that not only surrounds the physical body but extends through the emotional and mental fields. Practitioners begin by visualizing a core layer of the shield, a close layer of Arcturian energy that sits right at the skin's surface. This core layer acts as a primary filter, absorbing and neutralizing subtle influences that might affect the practitioner's thoughts or emotions. The process of layering gives the shield a depth and flexibility, allowing it to adjust its density and reach depending on the practitioner's need for protection.

Beyond this core layer, practitioners visualize an outer layer of protection, one that extends farther from the body, forming a larger boundary around their personal space. This outer layer serves as a buffer, a field that detects and deflects energies before they reach the practitioner. In situations of heightened energetic demand—such as crowded gatherings, emotionally charged events, or intense environments—the outer layer acts as a watchful guardian, filtering energies at a distance, allowing the practitioner to maintain their peace and presence without disruption.

Customizing the shield also involves setting specific frequencies within each layer. The practitioner may attune the core layer to a soft, soothing resonance, one that calms the heart and mind while maintaining alertness to external influences. This core frequency provides a sense of grounding and inner strength, making the practitioner less susceptible to emotional or mental disturbances. The outer layer, in contrast, can be tuned to a more active frequency—one that radiates with a gentle, yet assertive energy, a boundary that subtly repels any energy incompatible with the Arcturian frequency.

Through these customized layers, the practitioner begins to understand the shield as an extension of their own will and intention. The shield becomes both a boundary and a bridge, a flexible structure that can adapt to subtle shifts in the practitioner's energy or environment. This ability to adjust and refine the shield empowers the practitioner to move through various spaces with confidence, knowing they are safeguarded while also able to interact with energies that align with their purpose and well-being.

Reinforcing the shield in moments of vulnerability or intense interaction is essential to maintaining its strength and integrity. When practitioners anticipate situations where they may feel energetically exposed—whether in challenging conversations, public gatherings, or periods of heightened personal stress—they can prepare their shield with a brief ritual of focus. In these moments, practitioners hold the crystal close, closing their eyes to visualize the shield thickening, its layers becoming more resilient and radiant. They may imagine the crystal's energy expanding outward, filling each layer with renewed light and reinforcing the protective boundary around their aura.

In addition to reinforcement, the use of personalized mantras or silent affirmations enhances the strength of the shield. Practitioners often choose phrases such as "I am protected," or "Only energy in alignment with my highest good enters my space." These mantras, when spoken or thought with intention, resonate through the layers of the shield, adding a frequency of self-empowerment that elevates the shield's protective qualities. The combination of crystal energy and mantra creates a field that is not only resilient but alive with purpose, echoing the practitioner's intention throughout the layers of their personal space.

A final enhancement to the shield is visualizing it as a flexible, responsive entity—one that can adjust its thickness and radius based on the practitioner's environment. In familiar, safe spaces, the practitioner may allow the shield to soften and expand, blending harmoniously with their surroundings. In contrast, when entering energetically charged or unfamiliar environments, the shield can become denser and more concentrated, a firm boundary that filters energies with precision. Practitioners come to rely on this adaptability, sensing intuitively when the shield needs to expand or contract, responding to the flow of energy around them with ease.

The dynamic nature of the shield means it is always responsive, growing in strength as the practitioner's bond with the Arcturian crystal deepens. Over time, practitioners develop a seamless connection to this protective field, feeling it as an intrinsic part of their energy, like a second skin that moves and breathes with them. This sense of unity with the shield brings an effortless resilience, a strength that does not require force but flows naturally, a part of their presence that harmonizes with the energies around them without interference.

In cultivating this adaptive energy shield, the practitioner finds an ally not only in the crystal but in themselves, learning to sense and respond to their own needs for protection with grace and intuition. This evolving bond with the shield and the crystal becomes a journey of self-trust, an understanding that protection does not isolate but rather allows the practitioner to move through life's currents with a quiet, assured presence. The Arcturian crystal stands as a silent, steadfast partner in this practice, a vessel of cosmic strength and subtle guidance that brings the practitioner closer to their own inherent resilience, moving through each moment with the clarity and confidence of a shielded, centered spirit.

Chapter 8
Energy Harmony

Within each of us, there exists a symphony of energies—a delicate balance that shifts and sways with the rhythms of our thoughts, emotions, and interactions. Arcturian crystals, resonating with a unique frequency, hold the power to harmonize these energies, aligning the spirit with a tranquil, stable core. This harmony is not simply a state of calm; it is a balanced alignment that allows for clarity, focus, and a deeper connection to the self. When energies are harmonious, life flows more smoothly, with a subtle ease that influences both the inner and outer worlds. The practice of using Arcturian crystals for energy harmony invites practitioners into this state, a process of restoration and alignment that gently guides all aspects of being toward unity.

To begin working with an Arcturian crystal for energy harmony, practitioners often start by centering themselves, inviting the mind to settle and the body to relax. Holding the crystal lightly in one or both hands, they allow their breath to slow, creating an internal rhythm that mirrors the calming pulse of the crystal. With each inhale, the practitioner feels their energy field expanding; with each exhale, they sense any imbalances releasing, as though the crystal is drawing these disharmonies out and transforming them into light. The crystal's energy acts like a tuning fork, gently vibrating in sync with the practitioner's own rhythm, nudging it toward a state of equilibrium.

The concept of energy harmony encompasses more than simple relaxation—it is a practice of attunement, where each layer of the self aligns with the Arcturian frequency. The practitioner may visualize their aura as a sphere of light surrounding their body, seeing any scattered or chaotic areas within it dissolving into the soft, steady glow of the crystal. The aura gradually fills with this calming energy, stabilizing into a steady flow that feels unified and balanced. This visualization aids the practitioner in creating a cohesive field, one that is resilient and harmonious, allowing their energies to blend seamlessly, from the physical body to the highest spiritual layers.

The heart, as an energetic center, plays a pivotal role in this process of harmonization. By placing the crystal over the heart, practitioners can focus on bringing emotional energy into alignment. The heart center is often a place where disharmony originates, as it absorbs the weight of emotions, memories, and daily interactions. When the crystal rests over this center, its frequency permeates deeply, softly resonating through the heart space and dissolving any discord that may reside there. Practitioners often sense a gentle warmth or comforting pressure, as if the crystal's energy is soothing each layer of the heart, bringing a feeling of deep peace and unity within.

Breathwork can amplify this harmonizing effect, acting as a bridge between the mind and body, helping to distribute the crystal's energy evenly throughout the practitioner's being. A practice of "equal breathing" works especially well, where each inhale and exhale is matched in duration, bringing a balance that mirrors the crystal's even, stable frequency. With every breath, the practitioner envisions the energy flowing from the heart outward, filling every part of their being, smoothing rough edges and softening areas of tension. This breathwork weaves the energy into each cell, each thought, and each layer of the aura, creating a gentle, flowing harmony that permeates the entire system.

Another powerful method for achieving energy harmony is through visualization, where practitioners see themselves surrounded by a calming color that resonates with the crystal's frequency, often a soothing shade of violet or indigo. This color represents the essence of Arcturian energy, a hue that stabilizes and balances. As they focus on this color, practitioners imagine it washing over their aura, flowing through each energy center and creating a seamless field of unity. This visualization not only aids in harmonizing energies but also connects the practitioner more deeply to the Arcturian frequency, aligning their field with the higher resonance carried by the crystal.

For those seeking a deeper experience, working with the crystal to harmonize specific energy centers, or chakras, can further enhance alignment. By placing the crystal on individual chakras, practitioners can target areas that may feel especially out of balance. For instance, the root chakra may benefit from the crystal's grounding energy, helping to create a stable foundation that supports all other centers. The throat chakra, on the other hand, may absorb the crystal's clarity, aiding in clear communication and self-expression. As each chakra resonates with the crystal, it draws upon its energy to realign, creating a chain of harmony that flows upward from one center to the next, linking them in a balanced line.

Over time, practitioners find that working with Arcturian crystals for energy harmony not only creates inner peace but also brings about a deeper sense of clarity and purpose. When energies are in harmony, one's awareness expands, seeing life with a fresh perspective that is both calm and perceptive. This state of balance is not static; it is a living, breathing alignment that adapts and flows with each moment, an inner resonance that supports the practitioner in every aspect of their journey. Through regular practice, the crystal becomes a trusted ally, a point of connection to a frequency that continually renews and stabilizes, guiding the practitioner toward a life of harmony and integration.

The harmony cultivated through these practices reflects itself outwardly, influencing relationships, decisions, and the way the practitioner interacts with the world. As the energy field becomes more balanced, it acts as a subtle magnet, attracting situations, people, and experiences that resonate with this newfound peace. Life flows more smoothly, challenges are met with a sense of calm, and the practitioner feels anchored within themselves, able to navigate with a sense of unity and purpose.

Arcturian crystals offer more than temporary relief from the chaos of life; they provide a pathway toward a lasting inner harmony, a practice that sustains itself through each breath, each thought, and each moment of mindful awareness. In this state of alignment, the practitioner becomes a living embodiment of the Arcturian frequency, a harmonious presence in a world that is ever-changing, carrying within them a light that is steady, resilient, and deeply attuned to the essence of universal balance.

To live in true harmony, one must learn to cultivate this balance, not only in calm and serene moments but amidst the inevitable stresses and turbulence of life. Arcturian crystals provide a path to maintaining this balance, offering techniques that bring stability to even the most challenging situations. These advanced practices allow practitioners to not only harness the harmonizing energy of the crystal but to actively direct it, using its frequency as a tuning force to restore internal equilibrium whenever it is disrupted. Through these methods, the crystal becomes more than a tool; it transforms into a constant presence of harmony, a touchstone of peace that can be summoned in times of imbalance.

One of the key techniques for applying the crystal's energy in moments of stress is through rhythmic alignment, a practice that synchronizes the breath, mind, and crystal's frequency into a unified pulse. In this exercise, practitioners focus on the crystal's soft resonance, feeling its steady, quiet energy flow in tandem with their breath. They place the crystal over the solar plexus or heart center, feeling its weight as an anchor. With each breath, they visualize this center as a calm, luminous point of balance. The inhale invites the crystal's frequency into the body, the exhale releases stress, tension, or any sensation of discord, creating a rhythmic exchange that quiets the mind and anchors the body in harmony.

This practice is particularly effective during moments of emotional upheaval or physical discomfort, as it allows the practitioner to ground their energy without resisting or suppressing what they feel. The crystal's energy works subtly, creating a stabilizing field that holds the practitioner's emotions within a safe, balanced container. Each exhale releases a layer of tension, while each inhale fills the body with a gentle steadiness. As the process unfolds, a calm center emerges within, allowing the practitioner to observe their emotions with clarity, without becoming overwhelmed or swept away by them.

For those who seek an even deeper harmonization, Arcturian crystals can be incorporated into alignment rituals that attune the entire energy field. These rituals serve as a reset for times when the energy feels scattered or fragmented, drawing the practitioner back into alignment with the crystal's harmonizing frequency. One such ritual involves creating an "energetic circuit," where the practitioner lies comfortably with the crystal placed near the crown or root chakra. They then visualize a current of energy flowing from the crystal, through the body, and back to the crystal, forming a continuous loop. This circuit links each energy center, harmonizing them in unison with the crystal's frequency, until the entire field feels unified and whole.

Practitioners often report that during this circuit, they feel each layer of their being coming into sync, a sensation like a gentle wave that moves from head to toe. The body relaxes, the mind quiets, and the energy centers feel as though they are resonating at the same frequency, fully balanced and aligned. This alignment ritual not only calms the practitioner but deepens their bond with the crystal, creating a harmony that persists even after the practice concludes. As they return to daily life, they carry this balanced resonance with them, experiencing a heightened sense of connection, clarity, and calm in every interaction.

Another advanced technique for energetic harmonization involves working directly with stress points, those specific areas within the energy field that may hold tension or unease. To do this, practitioners scan their body, paying attention to any sensations of heaviness, tightness, or discomfort. Holding the crystal, they direct its energy toward these areas, visualizing it flowing gently into each point of stress, dissolving the discord like a wave that smooths jagged stones. Practitioners may imagine the crystal's frequency as a soft light or a cooling balm, one that moves directly into the source of discomfort, soothing and aligning until the entire field feels unified.

For more complex situations where energy feels dense or resistant, the crystal's energy can be reinforced with visualizations of harmony. In this practice, practitioners envision their aura as a fluid, flowing sphere that surrounds them, with the crystal at the center. They imagine this sphere glowing softly, expanding with each breath, radiating outward until it touches everything around them. The crystal's energy flows through the aura, filling each layer with the Arcturian frequency, creating a field that is both calming and resilient, a living barrier of harmony that prevents external energies from disturbing their peace.

Arcturian crystals also serve as powerful allies in moments of sudden stress, as their resonance can be invoked even without physical contact. For practitioners who have worked deeply with their crystals, the energy of harmony becomes an internal state, a frequency they can recall from memory and intention alone. In times of need, simply visualizing the crystal, recalling its energy, can bring a sense of calm and stability. This mental attunement, though subtle, draws the practitioner back into alignment, reminding them of the harmony that the crystal brings and the balance that resides within themselves.

With regular practice, harmonizing with Arcturian crystals becomes an effortless part of the practitioner's life, an instinctive response to life's fluctuations. This harmony is not static; it is a flexible, dynamic alignment that adapts to each situation, allowing practitioners to experience the flow of life with a sense of calm and clarity that extends beyond the immediate moment. Practitioners often find that, over time, their own energy field becomes attuned to the crystal's frequency, a living embodiment of harmony that sustains itself long after each session concludes.

The result is a profound internal peace that radiates outward, influencing not only the practitioner but their surroundings, creating an atmosphere of calm that naturally draws others into its sphere. The harmony within becomes a guiding presence, a state of balanced awareness that the practitioner can carry into every aspect of life. In this way, Arcturian crystals help reveal the quiet power of true harmony, a path that brings the practitioner closer to a life of effortless balance, rooted deeply in the resonance of the Arcturian frequency.

Chapter 9
Crystal Meditation Techniques

Meditation, at its core, is a journey inward, a practice that allows one to access the depths of self-awareness and explore the unseen layers of consciousness. When Arcturian crystals are introduced into this journey, their unique energy amplifies the experience, guiding practitioners into realms of clarity, healing, and insight. The Arcturian frequency within these crystals acts as a bridge between the physical world and the subtle layers of energy, making them a powerful ally in meditation. Through the gentle resonance of these crystals, practitioners can quiet the mind, open the heart, and tap into a deeper state of connection with the vast energies that lie beyond the physical senses.

To begin a meditation session with an Arcturian crystal, practitioners often start by creating a dedicated, serene space—an environment that invites stillness and focus. Sitting comfortably, they hold the crystal in one hand or place it before them, allowing its presence to anchor them. As the eyes close, the practitioner shifts attention to the sensation of the crystal, feeling its weight, texture, and energy. They take a few deep breaths, each inhalation drawing the crystal's frequency into their being, each exhalation releasing any thoughts or tensions that might cloud the mind. This simple act of breathing with the crystal establishes a connection, a quiet opening into the meditative state.

In the initial stages of this meditation, the crystal serves as a focal point, a grounding presence that guides the practitioner's awareness inward. By focusing on the energy of the crystal, practitioners can quiet their racing thoughts, centering themselves within its calm and steady resonance. They may envision a soft glow emanating from the crystal, a light that slowly expands to fill their entire being. This light brings warmth, clarity, and focus, creating an atmosphere where the mind can relax and gently release its grasp on ordinary concerns. As the crystal's energy surrounds them, they feel themselves entering a deeper, more serene state, where the silence of meditation becomes a gateway to inner exploration.

The use of breathwork enhances this connection, as breath becomes a vehicle through which the crystal's energy can permeate the body. Practitioners often use a technique called "crystal breathing," where they imagine the crystal's light flowing into their body with each inhalation, spreading into every cell, filling each corner of their mind. With each exhale, they envision any lingering stress or negativity dissolving, being replaced by the pure, balanced energy of the Arcturian frequency. This cyclical breathing anchors the practitioner in the present moment, uniting their breath, mind, and the crystal's energy into a harmonious flow that supports deep meditation.

As the practitioner settles further into this meditative state, they may choose to focus on specific areas of healing or insight. By holding the crystal near particular energy centers or chakras, they can guide its resonance into parts of the self that need clarity or support. Placing the crystal over the third eye, for example, often stimulates inner vision, enhancing the practitioner's ability to access intuitive insight. With the crystal gently resting on this center, practitioners may feel a soft pressure or tingling sensation, a sign that the crystal's energy is activating their inner sight, guiding them into a realm where answers and insights emerge naturally.

For emotional healing, holding the crystal near the heart center brings a calming and nurturing influence, one that can dissolve emotional blockages and restore balance. In this position, the crystal resonates with the heart's energy, creating a comforting presence that allows unresolved feelings to rise gently to the surface. Practitioners breathe into this area, envisioning the crystal's light flowing into the heart, wrapping it in a soothing embrace. As they breathe, the energy of the crystal helps release lingering sadness, fear, or tension, allowing the heart to soften, heal, and return to a state of openness.

Visualization is another key technique in crystal meditation, one that brings the practitioner closer to the essence of the Arcturian frequency. Practitioners may imagine themselves surrounded by a vast field of stars, as if floating within a galaxy. The crystal acts as an anchor within this cosmic landscape, its light a steady guide that links the practitioner to the boundless energy of the universe. As they visualize this scene, the crystal's presence helps them feel connected, as though they are part of a greater whole, a current of energy that flows through all things. This visualization brings about a profound sense of peace and unity, reminding them of their place within the universal tapestry.

For those seeking a more profound meditative experience, sound can be combined with the crystal's energy. Practitioners may chant softly or hum, allowing the vibrations of their voice to resonate through the body and blend with the crystal's frequency. This sound carries their intention, acting as a bridge between the conscious mind and the deeper layers of self. Each tone reverberates through the body, merging with the crystal's energy and guiding the practitioner to a state of heightened awareness. This combination of sound and crystal energy opens pathways within the mind, allowing the practitioner to access deeper states of meditation with ease.

With regular practice, meditation with Arcturian crystals becomes a journey of self-discovery, a path that opens new layers of awareness each time. The crystal's energy grows familiar, becoming a trusted guide that the practitioner can turn to in moments of doubt, uncertainty, or introspection. Through this relationship, the crystal becomes more than a meditation tool; it becomes a spiritual companion, a steady presence that aligns the practitioner's energy with the Arcturian frequency, creating a space of healing, insight, and transformation.

In this meditative state, the practitioner discovers the crystal's energy as a living presence, one that resonates within and extends outward, influencing the spirit, mind, and heart. The practice of meditating with Arcturian crystals brings more than momentary peace—it establishes a lasting sense of connection to the deeper currents of life, a sense of purpose and alignment that extends into every corner of the practitioner's world. As the crystal's energy infuses their awareness, they find themselves more centered, more compassionate, and more attuned to the quiet guidance that flows from within. This path of meditation leads them into a realm where crystal and consciousness merge, a journey that transforms each moment of stillness into a step closer to the heart of universal wisdom.

As the practice of meditation with Arcturian crystals evolves, practitioners find themselves drawn to advanced techniques that deepen their connection to both the crystal and the inner landscapes it reveals. These techniques amplify the crystal's energy within meditation, guiding practitioners to explore layers of consciousness that are subtle, expansive, and transformative. Through specific visualizations, breathing methods, and guided postures, practitioners enter states of awareness that touch upon the profound, tapping into a space where self and crystal resonate as one, harmonizing with the quiet, cosmic current of the Arcturian frequency.

One of the most powerful advanced techniques involves Arcturian visualizations that enhance the meditative state. Practitioners may start by imagining themselves within a sacred space—a tranquil, cosmic realm filled with soft, shimmering light. This space, while imagined, carries the frequency of the Arcturian crystal, a calm and balanced resonance that invites a sense of unity. The crystal, held in hand or placed nearby, becomes a focal point within this imagined realm, a beacon that guides the practitioner's awareness deeper into themselves. They may envision the crystal glowing as though it holds a piece of the cosmos itself, radiating light that flows directly into the practitioner's body, connecting them to the greater energies of the universe.

As the visualization progresses, practitioners might imagine this cosmic light streaming down through their crown, flowing gently down the spine, and pooling at the base of each energy center, or chakra. The crystal's energy guides this light, helping it flow smoothly, cleansing and aligning each center in turn. This alignment creates a sensation of ease and openness, allowing the practitioner to explore deeper states of meditation without distraction or resistance. Through this process, the practitioner's energy field begins to harmonize with the Arcturian frequency, creating a sense of spaciousness within, a clarity that feels as infinite as the stars themselves.

A more advanced breathing technique, known as "pulse breathing," can also be used to amplify the crystal's energy during meditation. In pulse breathing, practitioners take a deep breath in and hold it for a moment, feeling the crystal's energy radiating outward in small pulses with each heartbeat. As they exhale slowly, they sense these pulses expanding into their entire aura, creating a subtle rhythm that resonates through their body and energy field. This rhythmic breathing enhances the crystal's frequency, allowing it to permeate every layer of the practitioner's being, creating a deep and sustained state of meditative awareness.

Through this pulse breathing, practitioners often feel a heightened sense of presence, as though each beat of the heart sends a wave of clarity and calm through the body. The crystal becomes a part of this rhythm, synchronizing with the heartbeat, merging with the breath, and guiding the practitioner into a space where thoughts become quiet and the mind becomes a mirror of the crystal's calm energy. This practice serves as a reminder of the seamless connection between body, breath, and the energy of the Arcturian crystal, creating a harmonious meditation that feels as natural as the breath itself.

Another advanced meditation technique involves guided postures that invite a closer resonance with the crystal's energy.

Practitioners may lie in a relaxed posture, with the crystal placed over the third eye, the heart, or the solar plexus, allowing its energy to flow directly into these centers. In this position, the crystal's energy can interact directly with the physical body, encouraging relaxation, clarity, and balance. Practitioners close their eyes and focus on the sensation of the crystal resting upon them, feeling its gentle weight as an anchor that keeps them rooted in the present while expanding their awareness into more subtle realms.

As they remain in this posture, they may sense the crystal's frequency permeating not only their energy centers but the body itself, as though every cell is attuning to the crystal's calm resonance. Practitioners describe a soft glow that fills their body, an inner light that emerges from the center of each cell, creating a sensation of harmony that unites the physical with the spiritual. This deep resonance encourages a state of inner peace, where body and soul feel joined, and the experience of meditation becomes one of pure being, without expectation or goal.

For those ready to explore even deeper, chanting and toning can be incorporated to enhance the Arcturian frequency during meditation. Practitioners may choose a simple tone, like "Om," allowing their voice to blend with the crystal's resonance. As they chant, the sound carries the energy of their intention, filling the room with a vibration that harmonizes with the Arcturian crystal. This sound resonates through the body, connecting each energy center, and merging with the crystal's frequency to create a state of deep alignment. Practitioners often feel as though the sound reaches beyond them, connecting them to the broader cosmos, as though they are part of a larger symphony that extends beyond the physical space of the meditation.

Through these practices, practitioners discover that the crystal's energy opens doors to heightened awareness and subtle insights that emerge naturally in this expanded state. These insights may come as gentle intuitions, flashes of understanding, or a profound sense of calm that dissolves all sense of separation.

Each practice serves as a stepping stone, drawing the practitioner closer to a direct experience of the Arcturian frequency as it resonates through their own being, offering a glimpse into the depths of their own consciousness.

With time, practitioners find that this depth of meditation brings lasting changes, as though the Arcturian crystal has imprinted its frequency upon their consciousness. They return to everyday life with a newfound clarity, a quiet wisdom that subtly guides their actions and interactions, a part of the crystal's energy that now lives within them. This connection becomes a part of who they are, a resonance that they carry forward, an enduring touchstone of balance and insight.

Meditation with Arcturian crystals becomes more than a practice—it transforms into a relationship, a journey into the heart of awareness where each session offers a new discovery, a fresh perspective. The crystal, silent and steadfast, remains a companion on this path, a reminder of the peace and harmony that reside within, guiding the practitioner into realms of consciousness that are vast, boundless, and illuminated by the light of the Arcturian realm.

Chapter 10
Chakra Alignment

The body's energy centers, or chakras, serve as channels through which life force flows, influencing our physical, emotional, and spiritual states. These chakras, when aligned and balanced, create a harmonious energy field that supports well-being, clarity, and vitality. Arcturian crystals, with their distinct resonance, offer a unique pathway to chakra alignment. Their frequency aligns seamlessly with each chakra's energy, enhancing the natural flow and restoring any areas of imbalance. Working with these crystals not only strengthens individual chakras but also brings the practitioner's entire energetic field into harmonious alignment.

To begin aligning the chakras with an Arcturian crystal, practitioners start by setting an intention of balance and openness, inviting the crystal's energy to support the process. This intention guides the work, creating a focus that the crystal's energy can amplify. Practitioners often start at the root chakra, located at the base of the spine, and move upward, working through each chakra to establish a complete alignment. The root chakra, connected to grounding and stability, resonates with the crystal's foundational energy, providing a strong base that supports all other chakras. Holding the crystal over the root, practitioners visualize a deep red glow that flows from the crystal into the chakra, grounding and stabilizing their entire energy field.

As the work moves to the sacral chakra, located below the navel and associated with creativity, emotions, and sensuality, the Arcturian crystal's energy helps unlock any emotional or creative blockages. Practitioners envision an orange light pulsing gently within the sacral center, harmonizing with the crystal's frequency to release any stagnant energy. Each breath deepens this connection, inviting the crystal's energy to support emotional flow and creative inspiration, helping the practitioner to feel at ease in expressing their true self.

The solar plexus, a radiant center of personal power and confidence located just above the navel, is next in this journey of alignment. Here, the Arcturian crystal's frequency reinforces self-assurance and clarity, as the practitioner holds it close to the solar plexus. They may envision a bright yellow glow, a warm, empowering light that expands outward, reinforcing their inner strength and self-worth. The crystal acts as a guide, stabilizing this center and aligning the practitioner with a sense of purpose and presence, making them more resilient to external influences.

As the crystal reaches the heart chakra, the focus shifts to love, compassion, and connection. The heart chakra, located at the center of the chest, is a bridge between the lower physical centers and the higher spiritual centers. With the Arcturian crystal placed over the heart, practitioners imagine a deep green light flowing through this center, softening any resistance or tension. The crystal's frequency merges with the heart's energy, inviting healing, empathy, and balance. This practice opens the practitioner to deeper connections with others, while also nurturing a profound sense of self-love and acceptance.

Moving upward, the throat chakra, found at the base of the neck, governs communication and expression. The Arcturian crystal here brings clarity to words and thoughts, aligning the energy in the throat center with the practitioner's higher truth. They may envision a light blue glow surrounding the throat, a clear and open field that encourages honest expression and creativity. The crystal's energy helps clear any blockages in this area, allowing thoughts and emotions to flow freely, transforming self-expression into an act of truth and integrity.

The journey continues to the third eye, located between the eyebrows, the center of intuition, insight, and spiritual awareness. With the Arcturian crystal placed gently over this center, practitioners envision a deep indigo light, one that connects them to their inner wisdom and the Arcturian realm. This light enhances the crystal's resonance, activating the third eye and sharpening the practitioner's intuitive abilities. In this meditative state, they may feel a subtle tingling sensation, a sign that the crystal is activating inner sight and opening channels to heightened awareness and insight. This clarity allows the practitioner to see beyond ordinary perception, accessing the intuitive wisdom within.

The journey through the chakras concludes at the crown, located at the top of the head, the center of spiritual connection and unity. Placing the Arcturian crystal here, practitioners envision a violet or white light flowing into the crown, opening them to the divine and creating a bridge between the self and the cosmos. The crystal's frequency merges with this light, aligning the practitioner with the vastness of universal consciousness. This connection brings a profound sense of peace and belonging, reminding the practitioner of their place within the greater flow of life. In this moment, the chakras feel as though they are humming in unison, fully aligned and open, forming a conduit that connects earth and spirit, self and universe.

Each session of chakra alignment with Arcturian crystals reinforces this balance, strengthening the practitioner's entire energy field. Over time, practitioners find that their chakras become more responsive to the crystal's frequency, as though each center recognizes and aligns with its resonance naturally. The crystal, through its constant presence and support, becomes an enduring partner in this alignment, a source of stability that the practitioner can return to whenever they seek balance and clarity.

As the chakras align, practitioners experience a profound shift in their state of being. They feel a grounded sense of vitality, an openness in their emotions, clarity in their thoughts, and a heightened sense of connection to their intuition and spiritual purpose. This harmony within the chakras reflects outwardly, influencing their interactions, decisions, and responses to life's challenges. The journey of alignment becomes a cycle of renewal, a practice that nurtures both the energy centers and the spirit, guiding the practitioner toward a life of balance, peace, and spiritual attunement.

With each chakra attuned to the Arcturian crystal's frequency, practitioners discover that their energy centers do not function as isolated points but as a unified system of resonance. As the relationship with the crystal deepens, practitioners can delve into advanced practices that enhance this alignment further, ensuring a continuous flow of energy through each center. These techniques allow for a dynamic state of balance, where the energy centers support each other and respond in harmony with the fluctuations of daily life, creating a resilient foundation for physical, emotional, and spiritual well-being.

To cultivate a deeper alignment of the chakras, practitioners may begin with an extended harmonization ritual, a session where they engage each center with intention, directing the crystal's energy in a way that supports each chakra while simultaneously linking them. They start by placing the crystal at the root chakra, but rather than moving quickly from one center to the next, they allow time for the energy to sink deeply into each point, imagining the crystal's frequency forming a bond with each center before progressing. This pace creates a ripple effect, with each chakra opening in response to the energy already present in the previous one, establishing a chain of alignment that resonates through the entire body.

While focusing on each chakra, practitioners envision the crystal's energy not only balancing each center but creating a bridge between them. The image of a gentle, spiraling light may be useful here, one that flows from the root chakra upward, connecting each energy point as it travels. This spiral acts as a conduit, a path through which the energy moves freely, keeping each chakra linked in an unbroken flow. With each inhale, the spiral grows brighter and more pronounced, weaving the crystal's resonance into every layer of the chakras, creating a unity within the entire energy system.

One powerful enhancement to this practice involves combining crystals with complementary energies. While the Arcturian crystal serves as the primary tool, a second crystal, chosen for its harmonizing properties—such as a clear quartz or amethyst—can be placed at the opposite end of the body, creating an energetic balance between grounding and spiritual openness. This dual-crystal setup amplifies the alignment, with one crystal anchoring the physical energy at the root and the other enhancing spiritual flow at the crown. Practitioners often feel a heightened sense of stability and expansion, as though each chakra has found its unique balance within the greater whole.

In addition to harmonization rituals, practitioners can apply focused visualization exercises to keep the chakras aligned between sessions. One method involves visualizing each chakra as a lotus flower, each petal responding to the Arcturian frequency with a subtle movement, as though gently swaying with the crystal's resonance. Practitioners imagine the crystal's energy as a beam of light flowing through the center of each flower, creating a soft illumination that holds each chakra in perfect alignment. As the petals expand and contract with each breath, this visualization fosters a dynamic, responsive connection to the crystal, maintaining alignment even outside of direct practice.

Guided affirmations also serve as powerful tools in sustaining the connection between the chakras and the crystal's energy. Practitioners may silently or aloud repeat phrases that resonate with the purpose of each chakra, such as "I am grounded and secure" for the root, "I am open to creativity" for the sacral, and "I am connected to divine wisdom" for the crown. As each affirmation is voiced, the crystal's energy flows into the corresponding chakra, reinforcing its alignment and purpose. This practice merges intention with energy, embedding each chakra with a reminder of its role and creating a lasting resonance that supports balance and flow throughout the day.

For a full integration of chakra alignment, practitioners may end each session by creating a cocoon of energy around their body. With the crystal in hand, they envision a layer of light forming around their aura, a protective yet permeable boundary that keeps the chakras shielded from disruptive influences while allowing beneficial energy to flow freely. This cocoon, supported by the crystal's frequency, acts as an energetic filter, maintaining the internal harmony of the chakras even amidst external stressors.

Over time, these practices bring about a profound stability in the practitioner's energetic field. Each chakra becomes not only balanced within itself but harmonized with the others, creating a resilient foundation that supports the practitioner on every level. This sense of unity within the chakras radiates outward, influencing how they interact with the world, respond to challenges, and connect with others. The alignment with the Arcturian crystal becomes more than a practice; it transforms into a state of being, a calm, centered awareness that carries forward into every moment of life.

In this dynamic alignment, the chakras form a pathway for the Arcturian frequency to flow continuously, creating a bridge between the physical and spiritual aspects of the self. This bridge becomes a source of strength, one that grounds the practitioner in their purpose and connects them to the wisdom of the cosmos. Through the work of alignment, the practitioner transforms, becoming a vessel of balanced energy, open to the flow of life yet anchored within, moving with clarity and purpose within the harmonious resonance of the Arcturian crystal.

Chapter 11
Emotional and Mental Healing

The journey into emotional and mental healing with Arcturian crystals opens the door to a deeper, more resilient self. Emotions, though invisible, shape the way we see and interact with the world, and when left unresolved, they can settle into the energetic field, creating blocks that affect every layer of one's being. The Arcturian crystal, with its soft yet potent frequency, provides a gentle method for addressing these layers, guiding practitioners into a state of release, clarity, and renewed strength. As they work with the crystal, practitioners experience an unraveling of emotional knots, a shedding of burdens they may not have even realized they carried.

The first step in using Arcturian crystals for emotional healing is recognizing the energy held within the heart center. Many emotions are stored here—joy, pain, love, and sorrow. Practitioners can begin by placing the crystal over their heart, closing their eyes, and breathing deeply, allowing their awareness to settle into this center. With each inhale, they envision the crystal's frequency merging with the heart's energy, and with each exhale, any feelings of heaviness begin to lift, as though the crystal is absorbing and neutralizing them.

One effective technique for emotional release involves visualizing the heart as a soft, radiant light that pulses with each breath, expanding and contracting around the crystal's energy. Practitioners imagine any unresolved feelings as dark clouds within this light, releasing as they breathe, and transforming into a soft glow that becomes a part of the crystal's frequency. This gentle visualization allows for an organic release, where emotions surface without judgment or resistance. The crystal acts as a steady anchor, helping the practitioner stay grounded as they move through this vulnerable state of healing.

For mental clarity, the Arcturian crystal works harmoniously with the energy of the mind, where thoughts and memories often intertwine, creating a web of tension. To bring clarity to this layer, practitioners may place the crystal gently over the forehead, the location of the third eye, where it can resonate with the mental energy directly. They envision the crystal's energy entering the mind as a stream of calming light, dissolving mental clutter and allowing thoughts to become clear and organized. As the light moves through the mind, it washes away worry, distraction, and any repetitive thought patterns that no longer serve the practitioner.

This mental healing extends beyond thought clarity; it touches into a deeper state of perception, where intuition and insight begin to emerge naturally. Practitioners may find that as they hold the crystal here, their inner dialogue quiets, allowing an underlying sense of wisdom and calm to rise. This process brings the mind into harmony with the crystal's frequency, offering a space where mental chatter is replaced by peaceful awareness, a state where new perspectives can emerge. In this state, the practitioner becomes receptive to deeper insights and intuitive guidance, as though the crystal has cleared a path to their own inner knowing.

Combining breathwork with the crystal's frequency amplifies the effects of emotional and mental healing, creating a bridge between the two. Practitioners can engage in "cleansing breaths," where they inhale deeply, visualizing the crystal's light entering their chest, and exhale with a slow release, envisioning any tension or emotion flowing out and dissolving. This breathing technique integrates the work on the heart and mind, allowing the crystal to connect these layers, harmonizing the emotions and thoughts into a balanced rhythm. With each breath, a sense of release and relief grows, gradually dissolving the barriers between mind and heart.

For those seeking deeper emotional healing, working with specific memories or feelings can help target areas where emotional energy has been held for long periods. Practitioners may hold the crystal while recalling a specific memory, allowing the feelings associated with it to rise. They do not analyze or judge these emotions; instead, they simply allow the crystal to absorb and transform them. By gently holding space for the memory with the crystal's support, the practitioner feels a gradual softening, as though the crystal is lifting the weight of the memory, leaving a sense of closure in its place. The crystal's energy assists in this process, acting as a safe container that allows the practitioner to let go fully.

Affirmations can deepen this healing process, merging intention with the crystal's energy. Phrases such as "I release what no longer serves me" or "I am open to healing and peace" can be repeated as the practitioner holds the crystal close. Each affirmation resonates with the crystal's frequency, embedding the healing intention within the energy field. These affirmations guide the mind and heart, reinforcing a state of emotional clarity and mental calm, as though each word amplifies the crystal's effect, gently drawing the practitioner back to a state of inner peace.

In the days following a healing session, practitioners may feel the effects of the crystal's work continuing, as though the energy lingers, holding the space open for further release and insight. Some may experience an ongoing sense of lightness, a mental clarity, or even heightened awareness of emotions as they arise. The crystal's frequency acts as a reminder, an anchor that subtly guides the practitioner to remain mindful of their inner state, allowing them to release old patterns with ease and grace.

Through regular work with the Arcturian crystal, practitioners begin to experience a profound shift in their emotional and mental state. Old burdens fall away, creating space for new thoughts, emotions, and insights to flourish. This practice teaches resilience, not through resistance, but through release. As the mind clears and the heart opens, the practitioner finds themselves more in tune with their authentic self, less influenced by past experiences, and more present with the energy of the moment.

In this journey of emotional and mental healing, the Arcturian crystal stands as a quiet but powerful ally, an energy that neither rushes nor forces but patiently supports. The crystal's frequency harmonizes the inner landscape, guiding practitioners toward a state where their thoughts and emotions can coexist in peace, bringing them closer to the balanced, resilient state that lies at the heart of true healing. This transformation does not come from escaping emotions or quieting thoughts but from allowing them to find their rightful place within, as the crystal's energy leads them into a deeper state of self-acceptance and inner peace.

The work of emotional and mental healing with Arcturian crystals moves into deeper realms when practitioners approach it as a layered journey, allowing the crystal's energy to permeate the inner landscapes of memory, thought, and feeling. This process, gentle yet transformative, reaches beyond surface emotions to uncover long-held patterns, bringing light to areas that may have remained hidden. Through specific guided practices, practitioners can release repressed emotions, dissolve mental barriers, and cultivate a lasting sense of peace, using the crystal as a steady companion and guide.

One effective approach to accessing these deeper layers involves creating a healing sanctuary, a mental and energetic space in which practitioners feel safe to explore emotions that may have been set aside over time. To create this sanctuary, practitioners begin by holding the Arcturian crystal and closing their eyes, visualizing a peaceful, protective environment—perhaps a quiet forest, a sunlit room, or a space bathed in a calming light. The crystal becomes an anchor within this sanctuary, its energy forming a protective boundary that keeps the space clear of any disruptive influences, allowing only a sense of calm and trust to permeate.

Once this healing space is established, practitioners are invited to bring awareness to any emotions or memories that arise naturally. Holding the crystal close to the heart or forehead, they allow whatever comes up to do so freely, knowing that the crystal's energy is there to absorb and transform any heaviness. As they focus on the crystal's frequency, they may feel the emotions begin to shift, the weight of past experiences softening. Practitioners breathe deeply, letting the crystal guide them into a state of release, where old burdens gently dissolve, leaving a feeling of spaciousness in their place.

For repressed emotions—those that may be more deeply embedded—guided visualization with the crystal can facilitate the healing process. Practitioners envision each repressed emotion as a layer within their aura, like clouds or mist surrounding their energy field. With the crystal held over the heart, they imagine its light expanding outward, softly dissolving these layers as it moves through the aura. Each layer releases in its own time, transforming from dense clouds into clear light, lifting away and merging with the crystal's frequency. This visualization, repeated over time, allows for a gradual unfolding, revealing new layers with each session and providing the practitioner with a gentle yet powerful release.

To support mental healing, the Arcturian crystal can be combined with focused meditative practices that dissolve limiting beliefs or thought patterns. Holding the crystal to the third eye, practitioners bring to mind any thoughts that feel restrictive—self-doubt, worry, or habitual patterns that may cloud their clarity. Rather than resisting these thoughts, they allow them to surface naturally, observing them without attachment. They envision the crystal's energy flowing into these thoughts, as though its light is filling each one with a transformative energy, gently breaking them down. The thoughts soften, disperse, and eventually dissolve into the crystal's light, leaving a clear, open space for new and supportive perspectives to emerge.

For those seeking to address lingering mental patterns, affirmations can serve as a reinforcing tool within the crystal's energy. Practitioners choose phrases that resonate with the qualities they wish to cultivate, such as "I am at peace with my past," "I trust in my own strength," or "I am open to healing and growth." With each affirmation, they hold the crystal, letting its energy amplify the intention behind the words. The crystal's frequency acts as a conduit for these affirmations, embedding them within the practitioner's energetic field. Over time, these affirmations replace older patterns, creating a mental environment that feels clear, focused, and resilient.

Another powerful method to facilitate emotional and mental healing involves connecting the crystal's energy with the breath in a practice known as "soul breathing." Practitioners hold the crystal over their chest or place it nearby, breathing deeply and envisioning the crystal's energy flowing into their body with each inhale. As they exhale, they visualize any stress, tension, or unresolved feelings releasing from their energy field, dissolving into the surrounding space. Each cycle of breath draws in healing light and releases whatever does not serve, creating a steady rhythm that feels both grounding and liberating. With each breath, the crystal's energy becomes more integrated within their field, creating a flow of release that clears both heart and mind.

The Arcturian crystal's energy also enhances emotional resilience, teaching practitioners to approach emotions with acceptance rather than resistance. During meditation, practitioners may hold the crystal and observe any arising feelings—whether sadness, anger, or joy—without attempting to change them. They visualize the crystal's energy as a gentle support, one that allows each feeling to exist without judgment. This acceptance, reinforced by the crystal's frequency, nurtures a compassionate relationship with the self, allowing emotions to flow naturally, rise, and dissipate without creating inner resistance.

In the days and weeks following these practices, practitioners often notice a shift, a lightness in their thoughts and feelings as old patterns begin to fall away. They find themselves more in tune with their emotions, able to recognize and release them with greater ease. The mind feels clearer, less entangled in repetitive thoughts, and the heart feels more open, capable of experiencing and expressing emotion without becoming overwhelmed. The crystal's energy, having woven itself into the layers of the practitioner's awareness, becomes a quiet but ever-present support, one they can rely on whenever they seek emotional or mental clarity.

Through this journey, the Arcturian crystal reveals itself as a gentle yet profound partner in healing, guiding practitioners to access a sense of inner harmony that lasts beyond any single session. Its frequency does not push or rush the healing process; rather, it teaches the practitioner to honor each layer of their experience, transforming emotions and thoughts with a patience and wisdom that reflect the crystal's own timeless nature.

In this state of acceptance and release, the practitioner learns to navigate their inner world with grace, no longer carrying the weight of unresolved emotions or mental clutter. The mind becomes a clear and open space, the heart a place of gentle resilience, and the crystal, ever faithful, remains a steady guide. This journey of healing unfolds as a continuous path, one that leads not only to self-acceptance but to a profound sense of peace that flows into all aspects of life, sustained by the enduring presence of the Arcturian crystal's gentle light.

Chapter 12
Physical Healing

In the practice of physical healing, Arcturian crystals offer a unique support that resonates beyond the surface, reaching into the subtle layers of energy that influence the body's wellness. These crystals work by aligning the practitioner's energy field with their healing frequency, creating an environment that fosters the body's natural resilience and capacity for recovery. Each crystal session invites practitioners into a partnership with their own physical well-being, using the crystal's gentle energy to alleviate discomfort, strengthen vitality, and promote overall health.

To begin working with the crystal for physical healing, practitioners start by setting a clear intention. They hold the crystal in hand, close their eyes, and focus on the area of the body where healing is most needed. Whether it is to address specific pain, enhance general immunity, or restore balance, this intention creates a mental and energetic alignment, directing the crystal's frequency toward the chosen purpose. The practitioner may visualize the crystal's light flowing gently into the area of focus, allowing it to fill the space with a soft, warming energy that supports the body's natural healing process.

One effective method for using the crystal's energy in physical healing involves direct placement on areas of discomfort. For instance, if practitioners are working with joint pain, they place the crystal directly over the affected area, allowing its energy to enter deeply. As they hold it there, they take slow, calming breaths, visualizing the crystal's frequency as a soothing balm that surrounds the area, relaxing tension and relieving pain. Each breath invites the crystal's energy further inward, encouraging the release of any tension held within the tissues, promoting circulation, and bringing the practitioner into a state of calm receptivity.

For those seeking to support their immune system, holding the crystal over the chest or abdomen helps connect its frequency to the body's core functions, where vitality and resilience are anchored. Practitioners may close their eyes and envision a protective light surrounding the crystal, merging with the body's energy field and spreading throughout, fortifying the body from within. This practice strengthens the connection between mind and body, creating a conscious alignment where the crystal's energy enhances the body's defenses, creating a subtle but steady field of support that encourages balance and resistance.

In moments of acute discomfort, the crystal's energy can be amplified through a practice known as "pulse breathing." Practitioners place the crystal on the affected area, then take deep, rhythmic breaths, feeling their pulse in sync with the crystal's frequency. Each inhale draws the crystal's energy into the area, while each exhale releases pain or tension, allowing the body to respond naturally to the crystal's resonance. This technique brings immediate relief, calming both the physical and energetic body, and can be practiced anywhere, whenever the need arises.

Another powerful technique for using Arcturian crystals in physical healing involves visualizing the body as a field of light, with the crystal serving as a focal point that illuminates each area in need. Practitioners begin by holding the crystal over a specific part of the body, visualizing its light spreading from that point, connecting each area until the whole body feels encompassed in the crystal's frequency. This visualization helps create a feeling of wholeness, as though the body and crystal are harmonizing in a single field of energy, dissolving blockages and promoting a sense of well-being from head to toe.

Combining the crystal with affirmations further amplifies its healing effect. Practitioners may hold the crystal over the heart or a specific area of the body and repeat affirmations such as "My body is strong and resilient," "I welcome healing energy," or "Every cell in my body vibrates with health." As each affirmation is voiced, the crystal absorbs the intention, reinforcing the message within the practitioner's energy field. This union of word and energy creates a vibration that the body recognizes, aligning each cell with the intention of health and vitality.

For chronic conditions, working with the crystal on a regular basis helps maintain the energy flow necessary for long-term healing. Practitioners may hold the crystal at the beginning of each day, setting their intention for sustained wellness, and allowing the crystal's energy to permeate their body gradually over time. Through consistent use, the crystal's frequency harmonizes with the body's rhythms, forming a resilient partnership that strengthens physical endurance and promotes lasting health.

The effects of physical healing with Arcturian crystals are not limited to isolated sessions; they carry over into the daily experience, bringing about a state of ease and groundedness that enhances overall wellness. Practitioners may notice a subtle change in how their body feels—a lightness, a sense of strength, or a deeper attunement to their own needs. The crystal's energy, woven into their physical being, acts as a silent reminder of the body's capacity to heal, thrive, and find balance.

As the relationship with the Arcturian crystal deepens, practitioners learn to listen more closely to their body's signals, sensing where support is needed and using the crystal's energy to address these areas intuitively. Over time, the body responds with greater resilience, adapting to the crystal's frequency and sustaining a state of harmony and wellness. Through this ongoing practice, the crystal becomes more than a tool—it becomes a source of continuous support, a companion in health, guiding the body toward a lasting state of equilibrium.

In this journey of physical healing, practitioners discover that true wellness emerges from the balance of mind, body, and energy, an alignment that the Arcturian crystal helps foster and maintain. With each session, the crystal's energy becomes more deeply integrated, forming a foundation of strength and peace that permeates every aspect of physical being. This harmony with the crystal's frequency brings a steady, gentle healing that flows with the body's natural rhythm, guiding it toward its fullest, healthiest expression.

As practitioners deepen their work with Arcturian crystals in the realm of physical healing, they uncover techniques for targeted sessions that address specific body areas, creating an even more profound experience of restoration and well-being. These sessions offer a focused approach, allowing practitioners to channel the crystal's energy precisely where it is needed, facilitating physical comfort and resilience. The crystal's frequency, attuned to the body's needs, interacts with the subtle energy layers surrounding each area, creating a space where healing can reach into the very foundation of the body's structure.

To begin a targeted healing session, practitioners may choose to hold the Arcturian crystal close to the affected area, inviting its energy to flow directly into the space in need. Each session starts with setting a clear intention, whether it is to alleviate pain, support recovery, or nurture overall strength. Practitioners then visualize the crystal's energy as a light that enters the body, settling into the tissues, muscles, or joints, and filling the area with a gentle warmth. This warmth, while subtle, brings awareness and a calming effect, allowing the body's natural healing mechanisms to activate and respond to the crystal's support.

For those experiencing chronic pain or recurring tension, holding the crystal in a series of positions along the affected area creates a pattern of relief and release. Practitioners may begin by placing the crystal at one end of the area and slowly moving it across, as though tracing an invisible path of light. This movement allows the crystal's energy to work in layers, gradually addressing each part of the muscle, joint, or ligament, dissolving any tightness or discomfort. With each placement, the crystal's frequency reaches deeper, creating a cumulative effect that relaxes the area and restores a natural flow of energy.

Combining this technique with breathwork enhances the crystal's effectiveness. Practitioners take slow, steady breaths, visualizing the inhale drawing the crystal's energy deeper into the body, while the exhale releases any pain, tension, or resistance. Each breath moves the crystal's frequency further into the area, as though the body and crystal are in a continuous cycle of give and take, where discomfort is released and healing energy is received. This rhythmic breath becomes a conduit for transformation, creating a steady flow that brings a gentle but thorough relief.

For internal areas or organs, the Arcturian crystal can be held in alignment with the body's energy centers, allowing it to send its frequency inward. Practitioners may place the crystal over the solar plexus or heart, depending on the location in need, visualizing its energy traveling to the organ or internal area. This technique reaches the body's core, allowing the crystal's resonance to interact with the layers of tissue and energy that surround and support vital functions. As the crystal's energy permeates these areas, it creates a sense of ease, helping the body maintain optimal function and alignment, especially in times of stress or fatigue.

Guided visualization can further direct the crystal's energy in targeted healing. Practitioners close their eyes, hold the crystal over the area, and visualize each part of the affected space as surrounded by light. They may imagine each cell, tissue, or muscle fiber receiving the crystal's frequency, as though the light is gently infusing every layer with vitality and balance. This visualization helps the body recognize and accept the crystal's energy, creating a bridge between physical sensation and the energetic support that promotes healing. Practitioners often feel a soothing response from the body, a recognition that it is being nurtured, held, and restored.

In addition to direct placement, Arcturian crystals can be used in conjunction with gentle physical movement, aligning the body's natural rhythms with the crystal's energy. Practitioners may hold the crystal while engaging in slow stretches or gentle yoga poses, allowing each movement to deepen the crystal's influence. This practice connects the crystal's energy with the flow of the body, bringing relief to areas that benefit from both energetic and physical alignment. Movements are gentle, creating a rhythm that enhances the body's flexibility and ease, while the crystal works to release any energetic blocks within the muscles or joints.

For a more comprehensive healing experience, combining the Arcturian crystal with sound or affirmations can provide a layered approach to physical wellness. Practitioners may place the crystal on the body and vocalize soothing sounds, like soft humming or chanting, allowing the vibrations to merge with the crystal's frequency. The sound, carrying both intention and resonance, amplifies the healing effect, creating a field of energy that surrounds and supports the entire body. Practitioners feel this sound merging with the crystal's energy, as though both are working together to restore harmony in every cell, creating a sense of wholeness that extends beyond physical relief.

Affirmations can also accompany each session, as practitioners gently hold the crystal and speak words such as "I am whole and healthy," "My body is strong and vibrant," or "Healing energy flows within me." Each affirmation, spoken with intent, aligns with the crystal's frequency, embedding the body with a gentle reminder of its own resilience. This integration of words and crystal energy brings the mind and body into harmony, creating an atmosphere that supports long-term healing.

Over time, practitioners find that working with Arcturian crystals for physical healing transforms their relationship with their own bodies. The crystal's energy teaches the body to recognize areas of tension, imbalance, or depletion, guiding it to address these needs naturally. As the crystal's frequency becomes familiar, the practitioner learns to sense even subtle shifts within themselves, using the crystal as a trusted partner in restoring balance. This partnership grows with each session, forming a foundation of resilience that sustains physical wellness and promotes an enduring state of comfort and ease.

The journey of physical healing with Arcturian crystals reveals a profound connection between energy and form, teaching practitioners that wellness is more than the absence of discomfort; it is a dynamic state of balance, strength, and self-awareness. Through each interaction with the crystal, practitioners deepen their understanding of their own body, learning to listen to its signals, honor its needs, and nurture it with the support of the Arcturian frequency. This path leads to a lasting physical harmony that is both restorative and empowering, a state where the body and crystal together create a resilient and vibrant foundation for life.

Chapter 13
Energetic Cleansing of Spaces

The spaces we inhabit absorb and reflect the energies we bring into them. Over time, they accumulate emotions, thoughts, and unseen frequencies from our daily lives, which can create an atmosphere that feels either uplifting or heavy. Arcturian crystals, with their purifying and balancing energy, offer a potent method for cleansing spaces, infusing rooms with clarity and peace. Guidance here explores how to work with Arcturian crystals to clear out stagnant energy, creating an environment that feels fresh, supportive, and aligned with the practitioner's own energy.

The first step in cleansing a space with an Arcturian crystal involves a moment of quiet intention. The practitioner holds the crystal in their hands and closes their eyes, visualizing the space around them. They then set a specific intention, such as "This space will be clear and calm," or "I release any heavy energies from this room." This focused intention aligns the crystal's energy with the practitioner's purpose, amplifying its ability to purify the area. By directing this intention into the crystal, practitioners form a partnership with its energy, setting a foundation for the cleansing process to unfold smoothly.

One simple yet powerful method for clearing a room is to walk through the space with the crystal, allowing its energy to interact with each corner and surface. The practitioner slowly moves from one end of the room to the other, holding the crystal at arm's length and visualizing its frequency radiating outward. They may imagine the crystal's energy as a gentle wave of light, one that touches every wall, floor, and ceiling, washing away any stagnant or disruptive energy. Each step brings a sense of renewal to the room, as though the crystal's frequency is transforming the very atmosphere into one of clarity and balance.

The use of circular motion enhances this process, especially in areas where energy may feel particularly heavy. In such spots, practitioners can pause and gently move the crystal in a clockwise circle, as if stirring the energy with the crystal's frequency. This circular motion creates a vortex of cleansing energy, breaking up any dense or stagnant vibrations. Each rotation reinforces the intention of purity and refreshment, allowing the energy to flow freely through the room. The practitioner may sense an immediate shift in the space, a lightness that grows as the crystal's energy continues to move and disperse unwanted frequencies.

For spaces that require a deeper cleanse, placing the crystal at key points within the room can create a longer-lasting effect. Practitioners may select a central location or corners where energy often gathers and place the crystal with intention, allowing it to act as an anchor that continuously purifies the area. By visualizing the crystal's energy expanding outward from each placement point, they create a network of light that connects across the space, creating a subtle grid that maintains the flow of positive energy. This technique works especially well for rooms used for meditation, relaxation, or creative work, where a calm and clear environment supports focused intention.

To enhance the process, practitioners can incorporate breathing exercises that synchronize with the crystal's frequency. Standing in the center of the room, they hold the crystal, take deep breaths, and imagine each inhale filling the crystal with energy, while each exhale releases clarity into the space. This breathing practice allows the practitioner to act as a conduit, drawing the crystal's energy into themselves and releasing it outward, creating a unified field of pure, clear energy that permeates every part of the room.

For larger areas or entire homes, placing multiple Arcturian crystals in specific locations creates a powerful cleansing effect. Practitioners may position one crystal near the entrance to filter incoming energies and another in high-traffic areas to maintain balance. This multi-crystal approach creates a network, with each crystal contributing to a collective field of clarity and calm. As practitioners move through the space, they may sense the crystals working together, each enhancing the other's frequency, maintaining a continuous flow of positive energy throughout the environment.

Visualizations can further enrich the space-clearing process. Practitioners may close their eyes and envision the entire room or house as a radiant sphere, with the Arcturian crystal's energy filling it completely. They imagine any shadows or dense areas dissolving into light, leaving behind a clear, expansive space that feels open and refreshed. This visualization enhances the crystal's influence, turning the room into a haven of clarity, a place where both mind and body can feel at peace.

After cleansing, practitioners may feel the need to set an energy intention for the room, reinforcing the qualities they wish the space to embody. This intention could be as simple as "This room is a sanctuary of peace" or "This space supports creativity and clarity." Holding the crystal, they repeat the intention, allowing its energy to carry the message throughout the space. The crystal absorbs and amplifies the intention, embedding it within the walls, furniture, and atmosphere, creating an energetic blueprint that sustains the room's purity.

As practitioners continue to cleanse their spaces with Arcturian crystals, they cultivate an environment that not only feels clear but actively supports their well-being. The space takes on a harmonious energy, one that reflects and enhances the practitioner's own state, creating a home or workspace that is both balanced and uplifting. This ongoing practice of space cleansing becomes a natural part of life, a way to maintain clarity within the home and reinforce the relationship between one's inner energy and the spaces they inhabit.

With time, practitioners may notice that their spaces begin to resonate with the crystal's frequency, as though the room itself has absorbed and attuned to its energy. Entering the room feels like stepping into a field of peace and clarity, a place that both reflects and nurtures the practitioner's inner state. The crystal's presence remains, a quiet but powerful influence that keeps the atmosphere vibrant and aligned, ensuring that the space remains a sanctuary of calm, supportive energy.

Building upon the foundational techniques of energetic cleansing, more advanced practices are explored to harmonize and elevate the energy within spaces using Arcturian crystals. These methods offer a way to create an environment that feels deeply supportive, not only through periodic cleansing but also by establishing a continuous flow of positive energy that renews itself. In these practices, the Arcturian crystal's energy becomes a constant presence, imbuing the space with qualities that promote balance, peace, and vitality, sustaining the practitioner's well-being with every moment spent in its resonance.

One of the most effective ways to establish ongoing energy renewal in a space is to set up a "crystal beacon" within the room. To create this beacon, practitioners choose a central location—perhaps a windowsill, a table in the main living area, or a corner of an office—where they can place the Arcturian crystal with intention. This crystal acts as a focal point for the room's energy, its frequency gradually radiating outward to fill the space. By visualizing the crystal's light expanding from this point in all directions, practitioners can envision it forming a subtle yet steady pulse that maintains the space's clarity and harmony.

To amplify the crystal beacon's effect, practitioners may periodically recharge the crystal's energy, enhancing its ability to purify and protect the room. Recharging can be done by placing the crystal in sunlight or moonlight for a few hours, allowing it to absorb natural energies. As the crystal returns to its place in the room, it releases this renewed energy, reactivating the beacon's influence. Each recharge strengthens the crystal's impact, keeping the space vibrant and resilient, a place that feels continually refreshed and open.

In rooms where emotional exchanges frequently occur—such as living rooms, kitchens, or counseling spaces—practitioners can create an "energetic filter" using the Arcturian crystal. They hold the crystal near the center of the room and set an intention for the crystal to act as a filter, allowing only positive and beneficial energies to remain. Visualizing a gentle flow of energy moving through the crystal, they imagine it capturing and transforming any disruptive frequencies, releasing only light and clarity into the space. This energetic filter keeps the atmosphere calm and balanced, enabling smoother interactions and enhancing the sense of harmony within the room.

Practitioners may also establish "energy anchors" in the corners of a room to reinforce its energetic stability. By placing a small Arcturian crystal or another crystal with harmonizing properties in each corner, they create a supportive field that stabilizes the energy flow throughout the space. This field connects the corners in an energetic grid, allowing energy to move freely without becoming stagnant or chaotic. With each crystal anchoring a part of the space, the room feels as though it holds a balanced, structured resonance, one that provides strength and peace. This method is especially helpful in spaces where energy may fluctuate, as it sustains a steady environment that remains consistent and nurturing.

Visualization techniques further enhance the effect of Arcturian crystals in creating a harmonious space. Practitioners may close their eyes and envision a soft, white light filling the room, with the Arcturian crystal acting as the light's central source. They imagine this light expanding outward, touching every corner, wall, and piece of furniture, imbuing each with the crystal's frequency. Any lingering shadows or areas of dense energy dissolve into the light, leaving only a sense of clarity. This visualization not only purifies the space but also charges it with a palpable atmosphere of peace, making it feel both open and grounded.

To sustain this sense of harmony, practitioners can establish rituals for daily or weekly space-cleansing routines.

These rituals might involve holding the crystal and setting intentions each morning, or using the crystal to bless the space at the end of the week, thanking it for its support. Regular practice keeps the space energetically attuned, making it more receptive to positive intentions and reinforcing the crystal's role as a guardian of clarity. Over time, these rituals become moments of connection with the space itself, creating a bond that makes the environment feel like an extension of the practitioner's own energy.

In cases where a room may be exposed to intense or fluctuating energies, practitioners may create a "cleansing cycle" by placing multiple Arcturian crystals in a circular arrangement within the space. This cycle enhances the crystal's natural ability to purify, as the energy flows between the crystals, creating a field of light that continuously circulates. Each crystal in the cycle strengthens the others, creating a network of resonance that ensures the energy in the space remains clear and revitalized. Practitioners may sense a calming flow when entering this environment, feeling as though the room is continuously renewed by the crystals' combined presence.

For practitioners seeking a deeper level of resonance, combining Arcturian crystals with natural elements like water, plants, or incense enhances the cleansing effect. Placing the crystal near a bowl of water or beside a potted plant allows the crystal's energy to interact with these elements, creating an atmosphere that feels even more balanced. The water, acting as a natural conductor, amplifies the crystal's frequency, spreading it through the room, while plants absorb and transform any stagnant energy, releasing it as oxygen and vitality. The addition of incense, like sage or sandalwood, can also amplify the process, creating a multisensory experience that reinforces the crystal's purifying influence.

In these ways, Arcturian crystals become more than objects within a room; they transform into active participants in the environment, partners in creating a space that continually nurtures and supports. Each technique deepens the crystal's influence, helping it to maintain a steady flow of positive energy that evolves with the practitioner's needs. As the space absorbs and reflects this energy, it grows into a sanctuary that fosters inner peace, creativity, and a sense of wholeness.

With time and practice, practitioners may find that their space takes on a life of its own, resonating with the crystal's energy even in the crystal's absence. Entering the room feels like stepping into a field of peace, as though the space itself has learned to hold and emit the qualities that the Arcturian crystal brought forth. The environment becomes a source of grounding, a place where energy feels naturally aligned, supportive, and attuned to the practitioner's presence, a lasting harmony crafted through the guidance of the Arcturian crystal's subtle and timeless light.

Chapter 14
Creating Protection Grids

Protection grids, formed by the strategic placement of Arcturian crystals, create a shielded space that fosters both physical and energetic security. These grids channel the crystals' frequency into a structured, coherent pattern, fortifying an area against disruptive or draining influences. Through focused intention, practitioners can use these grids to create an energetic field that both repels unwanted energies and nurtures a sense of calm, making the space feel secure and aligned.

To create a protection grid, practitioners first determine the purpose of the grid and the type of protection needed. For some, the goal might be to establish a private sanctuary in a workspace, while others may seek to protect a home from external disturbances. Setting this intention is the foundation of the grid; the Arcturian crystals respond to this focused purpose, aligning their energy to support and sustain the protective boundary.

One effective layout for creating a protective field is the four-point grid. In this layout, practitioners place Arcturian crystals at each corner of a room or area, forming a square that defines the space's energetic boundary. With each crystal positioned, practitioners visualize the grid lines connecting the four points, creating an unbroken barrier that encircles the area. This visualized boundary holds the crystal's energy, amplifying the grid's protective effect and ensuring that any disruptive frequencies are kept at bay.

To activate the grid, practitioners hold a fifth crystal at the center of the area, placing it with intention as the focal point that charges and maintains the entire grid. This central crystal acts as the "heart" of the grid, generating a pulse that radiates outward, keeping the boundary strong and balanced. Practitioners may visualize this pulse as a wave of light or a gentle vibration that continuously circulates through the grid, infusing each corner with the crystal's protection. The placement of this central crystal establishes a dynamic flow, creating a field that remains responsive to any shifts in the environment.

In addition to the four-point grid, practitioners may experiment with circular grids for more fluid protection. In this layout, Arcturian crystals are arranged in a circular formation, often around the perimeter of the room or space. This circular design creates a softer, all-encompassing shield that surrounds the space without rigid boundaries, allowing the energy to flow continuously. Practitioners envision the crystal's energy forming a luminous dome over the area, as if each crystal in the circle emits a light that rises and meets above, creating a canopy of protection.

The grid's strength can be enhanced through specific activation practices. One method involves using a piece of clear quartz or another harmonizing crystal as a "key" to link each point within the grid. Starting at one point, practitioners move the clear quartz to each Arcturian crystal in sequence, visualizing a line of energy connecting each stone to the next. This motion creates an unbroken line of light that seals the grid, empowering the protective field and ensuring that the grid's energy is stable and resilient. Each link in this sequence strengthens the connections, transforming the grid into a single, cohesive entity that functions as one unified protective shield.

Breathing techniques further deepen the grid's effect, with practitioners using breath to strengthen their connection to the grid's energy. Standing at the center of the grid, they hold one of the crystals, inhaling deeply and visualizing the breath as a flow of energy that radiates outward to every point within the grid. As they exhale, they imagine this energy expanding and reinforcing the boundary, as though each breath is adding another layer to the protective field. This breathing practice binds the practitioner's own energy to the grid, creating a harmonious link that supports both the practitioner and the space within the grid's shield.

Regular maintenance of the protection grid keeps it vibrant and effective. Periodically, practitioners may wish to cleanse each crystal in the grid to clear any accumulated energy and restore its frequency. This can be done through exposure to moonlight, sunlight, or by using a smoke-cleansing technique. After cleansing, practitioners return each crystal to its designated spot, renewing their intention for protection. This ritual not only revitalizes the crystals but also reaffirms the grid's purpose, creating a sense of renewal and continuity within the protective space.

Over time, the protection grid becomes an enduring ally within the environment, adapting to the energy dynamics of the space and maintaining a steady field of security. Practitioners find that the atmosphere within the grid feels more centered, as though the energy itself has aligned to support peace and resilience. Entering this space brings a sense of comfort, a reassurance that the energetic boundary remains stable and responsive, a haven from external influences.

The experience of working with protection grids reveals the subtle intelligence of Arcturian crystals, as they respond to intention and purpose with a quiet strength. The grid becomes more than a configuration of stones; it transforms into a living field, one that continuously holds and protects the space it encircles. This connection to the crystals, nurtured through practice and care, brings a profound sense of trust, as the space evolves into a true sanctuary that supports both peace and purpose, ensuring that all who enter feel aligned, safe, and protected within its gentle embrace.

With a basic protection grid in place, practitioners can expand their understanding of grid work by exploring advanced techniques to deepen and sustain the protective energy. As they gain familiarity with their Arcturian crystals, they develop the ability to customize the grid to respond to specific needs or strengthen its resilience. These methods allow for a versatile approach, enabling the practitioner to create a grid that adapts to different environments and levels of energetic intensity. Through these practices, the grid becomes more than a static boundary; it transforms into a dynamic, living shield.

One method to intensify the protection grid involves layering the crystals, where practitioners add multiple crystals at each point within the grid. This layered approach enhances the grid's strength, as the energy from each additional crystal amplifies the grid's frequency. Practitioners can experiment with combinations of different crystals, selecting stones known for grounding, harmony, or repelling negativity, and arranging them with the Arcturian crystal at the center of each point. By visualizing the energy of each layer blending and rising together, practitioners create a protective boundary that feels more robust and comprehensive, reinforcing the grid's integrity.

To further empower the grid, practitioners can activate it with a specific energy pattern, such as a spiral or a wave, that moves between the crystals. With focused intention, they visualize this pattern forming within the grid, starting from the center and expanding outward, or swirling through each crystal. This visualization gives the grid an active quality, creating movement that discourages stagnation and repels disruptive energies with a continuous flow. Practitioners may sense this pattern as a gentle pulse or vibration within the grid, a living rhythm that adjusts to the energy in the room and ensures the grid remains flexible yet resilient.

Another powerful technique involves synchronizing the grid with the practitioner's own energy through breathwork and visualization. To do this, practitioners stand at the center of the grid, close their eyes, and take deep, measured breaths, inhaling to draw the crystal's energy inward and exhaling to release their own energy outward into the grid. Each exhale weaves their energy with that of the grid, reinforcing a bond between themselves and the crystals. As they continue this cycle, practitioners may feel the boundary of the grid expand and contract with each breath, responding to their presence. This practice creates a grid that not only protects the space but harmonizes with the practitioner's energy, adapting to their needs and creating a personalized sanctuary.

Adding intention-based rituals can also deepen the grid's strength. Practitioners may choose to incorporate affirmations, such as "This space is secure and grounded" or "Only beneficial energy may enter," as they set up or refresh the grid. Each affirmation imprints the grid with a layer of purpose, embedding the intention within the crystals. By repeating these words at regular intervals, practitioners reinforce the grid's resonance, creating a boundary that feels naturally aligned with their goals for the space. Over time, these affirmations accumulate within the grid's energy, adding a subtle layer of protection and grounding that sustains the space's security.

For those seeking a more responsive grid, the use of "key crystals" enhances adaptability. Key crystals are additional stones placed within the grid, which practitioners use to adjust the grid's energy in response to specific changes in the environment. Positioned along the grid's edges or between major points, these key crystals act as fine-tuners, allowing the practitioner to amplify or calm the grid's energy as needed. For instance, if a room is exposed to heightened external energies, adding a grounding stone like smoky quartz or black tourmaline as a key crystal enhances the grid's shielding effect. This adaptability provides flexibility, making the grid a responsive boundary that meets the space's shifting energetic needs.

Over time, practitioners may choose to establish a "programmed crystal" at the center of the grid. This crystal, after being attuned to the practitioner's specific needs, acts as the grid's core, holding the primary intention for protection. To program the crystal, practitioners hold it, set a specific intention such as "sustained protection and peace," and visualize the energy of that intention entering the stone. Once programmed, the crystal is placed at the grid's center, where it continuously radiates this intention throughout the grid. This core crystal becomes the grid's anchor, ensuring that its foundational purpose remains intact, even as the energy within the grid shifts and flows.

Maintaining and refreshing the protection grid further enhances its durability. Practitioners may cleanse the grid periodically, either by smudging it with sage or another cleansing herb or by removing and recharging each crystal under moonlight or sunlight. This process renews the crystals' frequencies, clearing away any accumulated energy and restoring their original clarity. By returning the cleansed crystals to the grid, practitioners ensure that the protective field remains strong, vibrant, and responsive to their needs, creating a continual cycle of purification that sustains the grid's effectiveness.

In moments of change, such as moving to a new home or rearranging a room, practitioners can relocate or reconfigure the grid to realign with the new layout. This adaptability allows the grid to grow alongside the practitioner's evolving environment, transforming the space into a supportive foundation that adapts to both personal shifts and external circumstances. Each time the grid is recreated or adjusted, its presence within the space becomes more profound, becoming an integral aspect of the environment that reflects and enhances the practitioner's intention for security and harmony.

Through regular interaction with these advanced practices, practitioners find that their protection grids evolve into fields of lasting support. The Arcturian crystals, originally placed as individual stones, transform into a network of resonance that works seamlessly together. The grid becomes a protective space within the larger environment, a sanctuary that is both receptive to the practitioner's needs and resistant to unwanted external influences. In this dynamic harmony, the grid's energy resonates as a quiet strength, a field of calm that anchors and protects with each breath and moment spent within its boundary.

Ultimately, protection grids crafted with Arcturian crystals reveal the potential for a space to embody more than just physical walls or furnishings; they become energetic structures that mirror the practitioner's intentions, reflecting a sanctuary of resilience, peace, and gentle strength. The crystal grid, with its flowing and responsive boundaries, brings the practitioner into an ongoing relationship with their surroundings, a connection that fosters both physical and energetic security, creating a living field of protection that adapts, supports, and endures.

Chapter 15
Spiritual Awakening and Higher Connection

Arcturian crystals hold a unique frequency that resonates with the layers of consciousness beyond the ordinary senses. They become gateways, guiding practitioners into realms where spiritual insight, expanded awareness, and deep connection to universal energy unfold naturally. In working with these crystals, practitioners embark on a path of awakening that opens them to profound self-discovery, touching upon energies and understandings that feel both ancient and deeply personal. Initial practices are explored for cultivating a spiritual connection through Arcturian crystals, preparing the practitioner for a journey toward elevated consciousness.

To begin this journey, practitioners engage in a focused alignment with the Arcturian crystal, recognizing it as a tool that both amplifies and refines their spiritual frequency. Sitting in a quiet space, they hold the crystal in their hands, allowing its energy to resonate with their own. Closing their eyes, they breathe deeply and visualize the crystal's light expanding outward, creating a halo of gentle illumination around them. Each inhale draws this light closer, while each exhale invites it to settle within, merging with the body's energetic field. This harmonization creates an opening, a space where the practitioner begins to feel more in tune with subtle frequencies, where the everyday self gives way to the realm of inner perception.

Setting an intention is essential for spiritual awakening with Arcturian crystals, as it aligns the crystal's frequency with the practitioner's purpose. Whether the goal is to explore higher states of awareness, connect with the inner self, or open to universal wisdom, the practitioner focuses on this intention, holding it clearly in their mind as they work with the crystal. With this focus, they mentally send the intention into the crystal, visualizing it as a gentle stream of light that moves into the heart of the stone, embedding their purpose within its energy. This simple act of intention turns the crystal into a beacon, one that guides and aligns their journey toward a deeper connection with the spiritual realm.

A foundational practice for using Arcturian crystals in awakening involves meditation. Practitioners place the crystal on their third eye or hold it close to their heart, finding a comfortable position and closing their eyes. They allow their breath to soften, feeling the crystal's energy merge with their own, creating a bridge to higher consciousness. As they meditate, they may notice sensations—such as warmth, tingling, or a sense of expansion—signaling the crystal's presence as it gently elevates their frequency. Within this meditative state, practitioners release thoughts and enter a stillness that feels boundless, as if the mind itself is opening into a vast, inner space filled with quiet, luminous energy.

Visualizations add a profound layer to this practice, helping practitioners deepen their connection with the crystal and expand their awareness. One effective visualization involves imagining the crystal's energy as a column of light that extends upward, connecting the practitioner's inner being with realms beyond the physical. Practitioners see this column growing brighter with each breath, as though it reaches toward the stars, connecting them with the universal field of consciousness. As the light flows upward, practitioners may feel a gentle pull, as if they are being drawn into a higher plane where insight and spiritual awareness flow naturally. In this heightened state, the crystal serves as an anchor, keeping them centered while their awareness expands.

Practitioners can also explore the concept of attunement, the process of aligning with the frequency of the Arcturian crystal in a way that feels like a "tuning" of their own energy. Holding the crystal, they visualize their own energetic field as a sphere of light, one that resonates with the crystal's frequency, gradually coming into harmony. As they attune, they may sense a subtle shift, a feeling of entering a different state of consciousness where they are more open to spiritual insights, more receptive to the silent wisdom that the crystal holds. This practice creates a resonance that remains even after they set the crystal down, a lasting connection that draws them gently into states of inner knowing.

A valuable addition to these practices is journaling, an exercise that helps practitioners capture insights and moments of clarity that arise during their sessions with the crystal. After each meditation, they take a few moments to write down any impressions, thoughts, or feelings that surfaced. The act of writing grounds the experience, allowing them to bring the intangible into form. Over time, these journal entries form a record of their spiritual journey, a map that reveals patterns, insights, and evolving understandings that guide them further along the path of awakening.

Breathing techniques can also enhance the process of connecting with higher consciousness. One technique, known as "crystal breath," involves holding the Arcturian crystal in the palm and taking slow, deep breaths, visualizing each inhale as an intake of the crystal's energy and each exhale as a release of any mental or energetic barriers. With each cycle of breath, practitioners feel themselves growing lighter, as though they are shedding layers of thought, attachment, or expectation. This cleansing breath creates space, an openness within, making room for the spiritual connection to unfold more freely.

Through regular practice, practitioners come to recognize the crystal's energy as a quiet but steady guide, one that becomes increasingly attuned to their inner journey. They notice a heightened sensitivity to subtle energies and an awareness that extends beyond the self, as though they are part of something vast and interconnected. This connection transforms not only their meditation but also their perception of the world, bringing a calm presence that remains even in the face of daily concerns.

As they deepen their relationship with the Arcturian crystal, practitioners often experience moments of profound clarity, where insights come unbidden, revealing truths that feel both personal and universal. These moments are glimpses into the greater field of consciousness, experiences that feel like touchstones on the path of awakening. Each session with the crystal builds upon the last, a cumulative journey that leads them into a deeper, more expansive understanding of themselves and their connection to all of life.

In this journey, the Arcturian crystal becomes a constant presence, a companion that subtly guides practitioners into states of expanded awareness and spiritual insight. The crystal, with its quiet yet profound energy, aligns with the practitioner's intention and attunes their consciousness to frequencies that foster growth, insight, and a profound sense of unity. This is the path of spiritual awakening—a journey into the heart of being, where the self dissolves into the flow of universal consciousness, a state of peace, clarity, and deep connection with the greater whole.

With the initial practices of spiritual awakening and connection in place, practitioners can further explore the depths of Arcturian crystals' energy to access even higher planes of awareness. Moving beyond foundational methods, they engage with advanced practices that open doorways to profound self-discovery, mystical experiences, and a deeper communion with the vast, universal consciousness. These methods elevate the experience with the crystal, guiding practitioners into realms where intuition flows freely and spiritual wisdom unfolds as a natural resonance within the heart.

One advanced approach to higher connection involves invoking a "spiritual pillar of light" through the Arcturian crystal. To create this connection, practitioners sit comfortably and hold the crystal at their heart center or third eye. They close their eyes and envision a powerful beam of light extending from the crystal, reaching upward toward higher planes. This light connects with the practitioner's energy field, expanding upward beyond ordinary perception, linking them to the expansive consciousness beyond the self. As they maintain this visualization, they allow themselves to feel held within this column of light, as if they are both grounded on Earth and elevated into a higher state, harmonizing the body and spirit as they enter a space of deep peace and receptivity.

In this elevated state, practitioners may explore guided visualizations or inner journeys. Holding the Arcturian crystal, they visualize themselves journeying through the light, moving inward and upward toward a space where divine wisdom and cosmic insight are accessible. This visualization can be approached as a journey through layers of energy, each one representing a different level of awareness, until they arrive at a realm where thoughts dissolve, and pure awareness remains. Practitioners may sense images, symbols, or impressions arising as they move through these layers, each one a glimpse into the greater universe, revealing subtle truths that feel both timeless and deeply personal. Each session adds another layer to this journey, unfolding a map of their own spiritual path.

For those who wish to enhance their connection further, incorporating breathwork with mantra chanting or toning can create a powerful resonance that amplifies the crystal's frequency. Practitioners hold the crystal close, breathing deeply, and vocalizing a tone or mantra that resonates with the energy of peace, unity, or love. Each sound wave merges with the crystal's frequency, creating a ripple effect that resonates through the mind and body, opening channels within that align with higher consciousness. This toning practice awakens dormant layers of the soul, leading to a feeling of harmony within, as though the voice and crystal together are opening a pathway to the spiritual realm.

Connecting with higher planes can also be supported through ritual offerings or gestures of gratitude. Practitioners may light a candle, place flowers, or offer other symbols of appreciation around the crystal, establishing a space of reverence before beginning their session. This simple act of gratitude opens the heart, making it more receptive to spiritual energy, and encourages a gentle expansion that aligns with the frequency of higher consciousness. Each offering serves as a reminder that awakening is a journey of both discovery and surrender, where the self opens to the guidance and support of the universe.

Practitioners may also deepen their spiritual connection through the use of sacred postures, aligning the body to receive the crystal's energy with greater intensity. Sitting in a posture that grounds the body—such as lotus pose or seated on the knees—brings stability, while the crystal, placed at the third eye or heart, elevates consciousness. This posture serves as a container for the energy, creating a channel through which the Arcturian crystal's frequency flows, steady and continuous, guiding the practitioner into a meditative state where they are attuned to a higher spiritual rhythm. The experience becomes one of both inner stillness and heightened sensitivity, a space where the practitioner feels connected to their higher self and the vast network of life.

For a more immersive experience, practitioners may incorporate breath visualization, imagining each inhale as drawing in cosmic energy from above, through the crystal, and into the heart. Each exhale, in turn, releases any resistance, grounding this divine energy into the body. This visualization creates a dynamic cycle that aligns the inner and outer worlds, bridging the soul and the universe through the crystal's frequency. With each breath, the practitioner becomes more attuned to the higher connection, allowing the crystal's energy to guide their awareness to new layers of understanding, where they encounter a sense of unity with all that is.

Journaling remains a powerful tool in this phase of spiritual work. After each session, practitioners write down any impressions, visions, or insights that arise. These entries create a personal record of the journey, capturing the unfolding wisdom and the subtle transformations that accompany each encounter with the Arcturian crystal. Over time, these reflections reveal patterns, connections, and teachings that inform the practitioner's spiritual path, as though the crystal is guiding them through a story of awakening that is written from within.

Practitioners may find that their sensitivity to energy increases, as though their senses extend beyond the physical world, becoming attuned to subtle layers of existence. This heightened sensitivity is a natural part of the spiritual connection, a reflection of the soul's alignment with the Arcturian frequency. Through these experiences, they come to feel an ever-present connection, a sense of divine guidance that remains with them beyond the meditative space. This connection infuses their daily life with a quiet presence, a sense of support that flows from the realms of higher awareness.

In these advanced practices, the Arcturian crystal becomes a companion in the journey toward spiritual awakening, a steadfast presence that anchors the practitioner in higher consciousness. With each session, practitioners come closer to their own essence, a space of peace, insight, and connection that feels both personal and universal. The crystal's energy, once perceived as external, begins to feel like an extension of the self, an expression of the deeper consciousness that lies within. The path of awakening becomes a continuous journey, a flow of expanding awareness that leads practitioners not only outward into the cosmos but inward, toward the heart of their own being.

In this unfolding journey, the practitioner reaches a space where awakening is no longer a destination but a way of being—a state of continuous openness, a living connection to the source of all life. The Arcturian crystal, through its gentle guidance, becomes a mirror of this journey, reflecting the wisdom, peace, and limitless potential of the awakened soul, a constant reminder of the unity that underlies all existence. Through this ongoing practice, practitioners find themselves in a state of quiet joy, connected to the world and beyond, in the timeless space of spiritual presence and higher connection.

Chapter 16
Strengthening Intuition

Intuition—the quiet inner knowing that often transcends logic—offers a bridge between everyday consciousness and the subtle realms of perception. Arcturian crystals, with their unique ability to resonate with higher frequencies, can act as a catalyst for developing this intuition, enhancing a practitioner's ability to perceive energies, insights, and connections that may otherwise remain hidden. Guidance is provided for harnessing the power of Arcturian crystals to awaken and deepen intuitive abilities, fostering a closer alignment with inner wisdom.

To begin working with Arcturian crystals to strengthen intuition, practitioners create an environment that supports calm focus and receptivity. In a quiet space, they hold the crystal gently, taking a few moments to clear the mind of daily concerns. Closing their eyes, they breathe deeply, allowing each inhale and exhale to guide them inward, inviting a sense of openness. They then visualize a soft light within the crystal, one that grows gradually, reaching out as if to connect with their own inner light. This light serves as a bridge, creating a gentle but powerful link between the practitioner and the crystal, attuning them to its energy and preparing them for intuitive exploration.

Setting an intention is essential for intuitive work with Arcturian crystals. Practitioners may choose intentions such as "I open to receive insight," "I trust my inner guidance," or "I am receptive to the wisdom within." They hold the crystal and silently repeat the chosen intention, feeling it resonate within the heart. This focus aligns the crystal's energy with the practitioner's intuitive desire, transforming the crystal into a partner that guides and amplifies their journey toward greater awareness.

One powerful method for developing intuition with Arcturian crystals involves third-eye activation. Practitioners hold the crystal at the third eye, just above the center of the forehead, breathing softly as they imagine the crystal's energy merging with this center. This location, often associated with intuition and perception, becomes more attuned as the crystal's frequency flows into it. They may experience sensations of warmth, tingling, or lightness, signs that the crystal's energy is stimulating the third eye. Practitioners let themselves settle into this feeling, allowing the crystal's energy to open and expand this intuitive center, creating a receptive space for insight.

To deepen the connection, practitioners can explore visualization techniques that enhance their receptivity. One approach involves envisioning the Arcturian crystal as a doorway to intuitive knowledge. As they hold the crystal, they imagine stepping through this doorway and into a space filled with gentle, luminous energy—a place where insights flow naturally. Within this space, they may find themselves sensing ideas, images, or symbols that represent guidance or understanding. Practitioners do not analyze these impressions; they simply observe, allowing the mind to remain still and receptive, trusting that whatever emerges will carry meaning that unfolds with time.

Breathwork enhances the practitioner's ability to merge with the crystal's frequency, facilitating a deeper intuitive flow. Practitioners hold the crystal near the heart and begin a slow, rhythmic breath, inhaling through the nose and exhaling gently through the mouth. They visualize the inhale drawing the crystal's light inward, filling the chest, while each exhale releases tension or mental clutter, clearing space for perception. With each breath, they enter a state of heightened awareness, one that brings them closer to the quiet presence of their own intuition. This breathing cycle grounds the practitioner, helping them remain centered and attuned to the crystal's subtle influence.

Journaling becomes a vital tool for capturing the impressions and insights that arise during these practices. After each session, practitioners take a few moments to write down any sensations, ideas, or symbols that surfaced. Even details that seem vague or ambiguous may hold meaning when reviewed later. This reflective practice reinforces the connection between practitioner and intuition, turning fleeting impressions into a record that reveals patterns and guides them further into self-understanding. Over time, these entries offer a roadmap of intuitive growth, a tangible reflection of the unfolding journey toward deeper awareness.

For those who wish to expand their intuitive practice, integrating meditation techniques with the crystal offers further development. Practitioners enter a meditative state, holding the crystal at the heart or third eye, and allow the mind to settle. In this calm space, they focus on a question or area in which they seek guidance, letting the inquiry remain open, without expectation. They invite the crystal's energy to respond, not through direct answers but as gentle impressions or sensations that may guide them to clarity. This meditative inquiry aligns the mind and intuition, creating a flow where insights arise naturally and without pressure.

Engaging in nature with the crystal brings an additional layer to the practice of intuition. Practitioners may take their crystal to an outdoor setting, such as a forest, park, or even a quiet garden. In this space, they hold the crystal, allowing it to attune with the natural energies around them. The combination of the crystal's frequency and nature's grounding presence often heightens intuitive awareness, opening practitioners to subtle shifts, sounds, and sensations that guide their perception. This practice fosters a deeper connection with the world around them, a sensitivity that reflects in their own intuitive awareness.

Through regular practice, practitioners may notice a subtle transformation in their intuitive abilities. They become more attuned to the energy around them, sensing nuances and insights that often go unnoticed in the rush of daily life. This attunement extends to their interactions and decisions, where their inner voice grows stronger, guiding them with a sense of quiet assurance. The Arcturian crystal, once an external tool, becomes a trusted ally that deepens their connection to their own inner wisdom, a presence that quietly and consistently amplifies their intuitive potential.

In this journey toward enhanced intuition, practitioners find themselves in harmony with a deeper rhythm, a knowing that exists beyond the confines of logic or reason. With each encounter, the Arcturian crystal reveals more of its potential, guiding them inward to uncover the layers of insight and understanding that reside within. Intuition becomes a natural part of their being, a state where the mind is still, the heart is open, and the spirit is attuned to the subtle language of energy. Through this unfolding process, the crystal leads them gently into the profound space of their own inner knowing.

Building upon the foundation of intuitive practices, guidance is provided for advanced techniques to elevate and refine intuitive senses. Working with Arcturian crystals, practitioners move deeper into a state of heightened awareness, where intuition becomes an effortless, natural flow. Through visualization, concentration exercises, and breathwork, they develop a sensitivity that allows them to perceive subtleties and patterns that remain hidden from the rational mind. This journey turns intuition into a trusted guide, a bridge to inner wisdom that supports growth, decision-making, and deeper self-awareness.

An effective practice for enhancing intuitive abilities involves developing "intuitive visualizations" with the Arcturian crystal. In a quiet space, practitioners hold the crystal to their third eye or heart, closing their eyes and visualizing a deep indigo light emerging from the crystal. This light expands outward, filling the mind's inner space with a vivid, receptive energy. In this visualization, they imagine the crystal as a doorway to their intuitive center, a portal through which insights, symbols, and guidance can emerge. Practitioners observe any impressions that arise, allowing them to flow naturally without analysis or judgment, creating a space for deeper insights to take shape.

Advanced intuitive work with Arcturian crystals can also include specific exercises for activating the "third-eye breath." This technique combines breathwork with mental focus, amplifying the connection between the crystal and the third-eye center. Practitioners hold the crystal at the third eye, breathing in deeply through the nose and envisioning the breath entering the space between the eyebrows. On each exhale, they release the breath gently, imagining any mental clutter or tension dissolving. With each inhale, they invite clarity, and with each exhale, they expand their capacity to perceive. As the breath cycle continues, the crystal's energy aligns with the practitioner's focus, creating a powerful attunement to subtle awareness. This process opens the pathway to intuitive perception, a flow of gentle insights that feels clear, calm, and deeply present.

Another effective method involves "guided inquiry" with the Arcturian crystal. Practitioners hold the crystal and set a specific question or intention, one that relates to an area in which they seek clarity or guidance. They do not expect direct answers but instead invite impressions, images, or sensations that might offer insight. After setting the inquiry, practitioners sit in stillness, holding the crystal close, breathing slowly, and listening within. Through this process, answers often emerge in the form of feelings, flashes of insight, or symbols that resonate with the practitioner's deeper knowing. The inquiry session is not about logical analysis; instead, it involves a surrender to the crystal's subtle influence, allowing intuitive understanding to unfold on its own terms.

Visualizing a flow of energy from the crystal to the third eye is an especially effective practice for deepening intuition. Practitioners imagine the Arcturian crystal emitting a gentle beam of light that reaches their third eye, connecting the two. They see this light as a stream of clarity and insight, allowing it to permeate their mind, dissolving any resistance or overthinking. As the light connects the crystal to the third eye, practitioners experience an effortless alignment, one that opens them to receive impressions and understandings without effort. This visualization strengthens the mind's receptivity, enabling them to perceive nuances and details that may otherwise remain obscured.

Advanced practitioners may find it helpful to integrate Arcturian crystal practices into their daily routines, turning moments of reflection or decision-making into intuitive exercises. When faced with choices or challenges, they can pause, hold the crystal, and focus on grounding their awareness. With the crystal's energy amplifying their inner clarity, they center their attention on the decision or issue, listening for subtle impressions or "gut feelings" that rise in response. This daily interaction with intuition builds confidence in the process, transforming intuition from an occasional insight into a continuous, reliable companion in their daily life.

Regular journaling remains a central aspect of refining intuition. Practitioners write down any impressions or sensations experienced during their intuitive work, allowing them to review and recognize patterns over time. This record becomes a guide, revealing the evolution of their intuitive abilities and providing valuable insights that may only be understood fully in hindsight. Each entry builds upon the last, creating a personal guidebook to their journey with the crystal and their growing ability to trust in their own inner knowing.

Practitioners can further enhance their intuition by incorporating a simple yet powerful "evening reflection" ritual with the crystal. At the close of each day, they hold the crystal and briefly review the day's events, interactions, and moments of decision. As they reflect, they ask themselves if any intuitive insights arose throughout the day, even those they might not have consciously recognized at the time. Holding the crystal, they express gratitude for any guidance received, reinforcing their connection to intuitive wisdom. This evening ritual builds an ongoing awareness of intuition, making it a natural part of their perception.

When applied consistently, these advanced practices reveal a richer dimension of intuition, one that feels seamless and deeply integrated. Practitioners find themselves more attuned to energy and meaning in all situations, able to sense subtle shifts or unspoken truths with a clarity that bypasses rational thought. Intuition becomes less about flashes of insight and more about a constant, steady knowing, a sense of alignment that underpins their perception. Through the crystal's influence, practitioners gain access to this expanded awareness, where guidance arises naturally, without force or analysis, as an expression of the intuitive mind itself.

In this journey, the Arcturian crystal becomes a trusted ally, a tool that invites practitioners to reach beyond the boundaries of ordinary thought and into a realm of inner clarity and insight. The crystal's energy is gentle but transformative, opening pathways to intuition that continue to develop and expand, revealing new depths of understanding. Intuition, in this context, is no longer a mystery; it becomes a familiar rhythm, a state of awareness that is as natural as breath, guiding practitioners toward an experience of wisdom that feels both profound and effortlessly accessible.

Chapter 17
Desire Manifestation

In the realm of Arcturian crystals, desire is more than a wish or fleeting thought; it is an energetic pulse that aligns with the universe's creative force. By working with these crystals, practitioners learn to manifest their desires consciously, aligning their intentions with the Arcturian frequency. The crystal serves as an amplifier, transforming internal goals into powerful, directed energies that move out into the world, weaving desire into reality. Foundational practices are introduced to connect the energy of desire with the crystal, creating a clear pathway from intention to manifestation.

To begin the manifestation process, practitioners center themselves and focus on defining their desires with clarity and purpose. Holding the Arcturian crystal close, they close their eyes and allow the mind to settle, releasing distractions. In this quiet space, they ask themselves what they truly wish to bring into their life, observing as the desire becomes a clear image, feeling, or thought. This clarity transforms the desire from an abstract notion into a purposeful energy, an intention that they will imprint onto the crystal, empowering it to support and amplify their goal.

Setting an intention with the crystal is an essential part of this practice. Practitioners hold the crystal in both hands, directing their focus inward. With eyes closed, they visualize the desire as a bright light within their heart, a radiant energy that represents their goal or aspiration. With each breath, they see this light expanding and growing stronger. When they feel ready, they mentally project this light from their heart into the crystal, envisioning it merging with the crystal's energy. This moment marks the beginning of the manifestation process, as the crystal now holds and amplifies the intention, ready to support its unfolding.

A practice that further enhances manifestation involves creating a "manifestation mantra." Practitioners choose a simple affirmation that encapsulates their desire, such as "I attract success and fulfillment" or "My life aligns with joy and purpose." Holding the crystal, they repeat this mantra slowly, allowing each word to resonate within them. With each repetition, they envision the mantra's energy merging with the crystal, transforming it into a vessel that holds their words and intentions. This process creates a resonance between the crystal, the mantra, and the practitioner's own energy, strengthening the vibrational connection between their desire and its manifestation.

Visualization is another powerful tool in this journey. Practitioners sit comfortably with the crystal, closing their eyes and visualizing a scene in which their desire has already come to fruition. They see, feel, and experience this reality as though it is already present, engaging all senses to make the visualization as vivid as possible. In their mind's eye, they see the Arcturian crystal emitting light, a gentle, pulsing energy that surrounds and supports this desired reality. As they hold this vision, they allow a sense of gratitude to arise, feeling appreciation for the fulfillment of their desire as if it has already happened. This gratitude grounds the energy of manifestation, anchoring it within the present moment and aligning it with the flow of universal creation.

A grounding practice can amplify these efforts by creating stability, anchoring the intention within the practitioner's life. Practitioners may place the crystal on the ground or hold it close to the earth, envisioning their desire as roots growing deep into the ground, connecting to the stability and support of the earth itself. This grounding process roots the desire firmly in reality, transforming it from a vision into something that feels tangible and achievable. As they feel this connection, practitioners experience a sense of calm confidence, a knowing that their desire is supported by both the crystal's energy and the earth's strength.

To reinforce the manifestation process, practitioners can create a "sacred space" where they keep the crystal and any symbols related to their desire. This space could be a small altar, a shelf, or a specific corner where the crystal remains undisturbed, its energy radiating outward. Placing symbols, such as images, words, or objects that relate to the desire, around the crystal, they create a focused environment that nurtures their intention. Each time they visit this space, they feel a renewed connection to their goal, as though the crystal is a silent, constant ally supporting their journey.

In daily life, practitioners can also enhance manifestation through brief moments of reconnection. Throughout the day, they take a few seconds to place a hand over the heart, silently affirming their intention or desire. By linking this practice with the crystal's energy, they create a steady thread of focus that keeps them aligned with their goal. This continual awareness fosters a resilient connection between the practitioner and their desire, reminding them of the crystal's presence and reinforcing the commitment to their goal.

As they engage with these practices, practitioners begin to notice subtle shifts within themselves and their surroundings. They become more aware of opportunities, feel a deeper sense of alignment, and trust the natural unfolding of their desire. The Arcturian crystal, once just a supportive tool, becomes an extension of their intention, a partner in the creative process that bridges the space between thought and reality.

In the end, working with the Arcturian crystal for manifestation is more than a simple exercise in visualization or desire. It becomes a journey of conscious co-creation, an experience where the practitioner learns to align with their own inner power, grounded in the wisdom and energy of the crystal. Each step, each affirmation, and each visualization becomes part of a greater flow, moving the practitioner closer to realizing their deepest aspirations with quiet confidence and trust in the process.

Through these practices, the Arcturian crystal not only supports desire but transforms it into an active, living force that shapes their path and manifests their dreams into reality.

As practitioners deepen their work with Arcturian crystals in manifesting their desires, they explore advanced techniques that strengthen the alignment between their inner world and their goals. By integrating visualization, intention, and energy alignment, they move beyond simply focusing on outcomes. Instead, they learn to resonate with the frequency of their desires as if they already exist, anchoring them more fully in both mind and spirit. Further guidance is provided on refining these manifestation practices, making the process not only intentional but also energetically powerful.

To amplify the manifestation process, practitioners begin by setting a daily ritual with the crystal. They hold the crystal close each morning, allowing its energy to merge with their own, setting an intention for how they wish to move through the day in alignment with their goals. In this practice, they don't focus solely on achieving a particular outcome; rather, they concentrate on embodying the qualities, feelings, or mindsets that their desire represents. By setting this daily ritual, practitioners gradually weave their intentions into the fabric of their everyday life, aligning their thoughts, actions, and emotions with their ultimate goal.

A powerful addition to manifestation practices is the use of "energetic affirmations," where practitioners repeat phrases that embody the essence of their desire. For instance, instead of simply affirming "I am successful," they could use "I feel the presence of success growing within me each day." Holding the Arcturian crystal, they repeat the affirmation with conviction, feeling it resonate through the body. This shifts their energy into alignment with the desired state. Practitioners might visualize the crystal absorbing the affirmation, amplifying its power and radiating it outward, as though the crystal is a broadcasting center for their intention.

Another transformative technique involves creating "energetic blueprints" with the crystal, a visualization that expands on simple desire. Practitioners begin by holding the crystal and entering a meditative state. They then picture their life not only with the desired outcome achieved but also envisioning the ripple effects it brings into various aspects of their life. They allow themselves to feel the atmosphere, sounds, and colors in this imagined future, focusing on the connections, experiences, and sensations that their manifested desire would create. By involving all senses, they are not just envisioning an isolated goal but creating a comprehensive blueprint of their future that the crystal supports in making real.

The "mirror technique" offers another advanced method for cultivating the energy of manifestation. In a quiet space, practitioners sit before a mirror with the Arcturian crystal in hand. They look directly at their own reflection, connecting with their own gaze, while holding the crystal as a grounding source of support. Speaking aloud, they affirm statements as if their desire is already fulfilled. "I am living my dream," "I am surrounded by opportunities," or "I am abundant in all ways." As they speak, they observe the sincerity in their own eyes, allowing the crystal's energy to strengthen their self-belief. This practice builds a resonance between their current self and the version of themselves that has already achieved the desired reality, grounding the manifestation further in self-trust and intention.

To intensify the effect, practitioners can engage in a focused energy release ritual with the Arcturian crystal. This involves gathering the crystal and any other objects that represent their desire—a symbolic item, a written affirmation, or a personal belonging. In a meditative state, they hold the crystal over these items and visualize a beam of energy connecting them all, infusing each item with the same purpose. Then, they "release" the energy, imagining it flowing outward from the crystal into the world, carrying their intention into the collective energy field where it can attract circumstances and alignments that support their desire. This release shifts the energy from internal intention to external action, a movement that serves as a bridge between thought and reality.

Using gratitude as a cornerstone, practitioners anchor the manifestation in present awareness. Each day, they take a moment with the crystal, expressing appreciation not only for the potential realization of their goal but for each small step, insight, or opportunity that brings them closer to it. They hold the crystal, thanking it as if the desire has already manifested, feeling this gratitude expand from their heart outward. This gratitude resonates with the crystal, creating a feedback loop of positive energy that maintains a high vibration, attracting more of what they seek. Through gratitude, practitioners align with the flow of receiving, trusting the unfolding of their goal.

Another tool that enhances manifestation with the Arcturian crystal is the creation of a "vision scroll." Practitioners write their goals, affirmations, or desired outcomes on a piece of paper, infusing it with intention. Rolling the paper, they place it beside or beneath the crystal, where it will remain in their sacred space. Each time they pass this space or pause before the crystal, they reinforce the connection to their desires, adding a subtle layer of energy to the intention. This scroll serves as a physical reminder, a tether between the goal and their everyday reality, integrating the manifestation into their consciousness as an ongoing journey.

As they immerse themselves in these practices, practitioners start to experience subtle changes, not just externally, but in their own sense of presence and purpose. They become attuned to the energy surrounding their goals, more perceptive to signs, symbols, and opportunities that align with their path. The Arcturian crystal becomes a trusted ally in this journey, amplifying each intention, creating a clear channel through which desires flow from thought to form.

In time, practitioners find that manifestation becomes a natural part of their awareness, a process that feels less like striving and more like alignment. The desires they hold become an extension of their own frequency, resonating as an authentic expression of who they are. Working with the Arcturian crystal in this way turns manifestation from a singular act into a way of life, an ongoing connection between their internal aspirations and the universe's response.

Through this powerful alliance with the crystal, practitioners discover that they are not simply pursuing desires; they are creating a lived experience that embodies purpose, joy, and fulfillment. With the crystal as both a guide and a conduit, they enter a flow where intention transforms into reality, weaving desire into the fabric of existence with clarity, strength, and unwavering trust in the natural unfolding of their dreams.

Chapter 18
Sacred Space

A sacred space is more than a physical location; it is an environment charged with intention and aligned with one's highest energy. Creating such a space with Arcturian crystals allows practitioners to establish a place of sanctuary where they can reconnect with their inner self, focus their spiritual practices, and feel protected from external influences. The sacred space becomes a tangible expression of inner peace and alignment, a setting where the practitioner's intentions, goals, and personal energy harmonize. Foundational steps are introduced for creating a sacred space using Arcturian crystals, transforming an area in the home or personal space into a powerful environment for spiritual work.

The first step in establishing a sacred space is choosing a location that feels energetically receptive, calm, and private. Practitioners explore their living spaces, observing the natural energy of each room, and select a corner, alcove, or shelf that feels open and peaceful. If possible, they choose a space that receives natural light or has a view of nature, as these elements can enhance the flow of positive energy within the area. Once the space is chosen, they clear any unnecessary objects, ensuring the area feels open and uncluttered, a blank canvas ready to be infused with their intention.

To prepare the space energetically, practitioners begin by cleansing it. They might use smudging techniques with sage, palo santo, or other cleansing herbs, allowing the smoke to drift through the area, removing any stagnant or unwanted energy. If smoke cleansing isn't possible, they can sprinkle salt in the corners of the space or place a bowl of water infused with a few drops of essential oils like lavender or rosemary to cleanse and refresh. As they cleanse, they focus on the intention to create a sanctuary, a place of quiet and connection. This cleansing ritual prepares the space to receive the Arcturian crystal, transforming it into a blank slate where new energy can flourish.

Placing the Arcturian crystal is a central act in creating the sacred space. Practitioners select one or several crystals that resonate with the purpose of the space—whether for meditation, healing, manifestation, or general peace. They hold the crystal, focusing on their intention for the space, allowing the crystal to absorb this intention. With care, they place it in a central location within the space, envisioning the crystal as a source of light and energy that fills the entire area. This placement anchors the crystal's frequency, setting a foundation upon which the sacred space can be built, resonating with the Arcturian energy that supports and protects the practitioner's journey.

Enhancing the space further involves incorporating items that reflect the practitioner's spiritual focus and personal intentions. They may add elements such as candles, which represent illumination and clarity, or flowers and plants, symbols of life and growth. Each item is chosen with purpose, added with the understanding that it contributes its energy to the space. For example, a piece of fabric in a color associated with peace or grounding might cover the area where the crystal rests, creating a soft, inviting atmosphere. The practitioner arranges these objects in a way that feels natural and harmonious, focusing on simplicity and the flow of energy, allowing the area to evolve as a personal sanctuary.

A powerful practice for imbuing the space with energy involves creating a daily ritual with the Arcturian crystal. Each morning or evening, practitioners visit the space, holding the crystal and taking a few moments to ground themselves. They close their eyes, breathe deeply, and envision the crystal's energy expanding, filling the space with a calming light that creates a gentle boundary around them. As they breathe, they feel their own energy aligning with the space, sensing a connection that grows stronger with each visit. This ritual not only empowers the space but also helps the practitioner build a steady, peaceful presence that remains with them even outside the sacred area.

Including personal symbols or items that hold special meaning enhances the space's resonance. These symbols could be objects like family heirlooms, photographs, or small tokens that remind the practitioner of significant experiences or loved ones. Placing these objects with the Arcturian crystal deepens the connection to the space, as each item adds an emotional and energetic layer. These symbols create a sense of continuity, reminding the practitioner of their values, intentions, and journey, transforming the space into a mirror of their inner life.

Practitioners can also experiment with adding natural elements to balance the energy in the sacred space. Stones, feathers, seashells, or small bowls of water introduce Earth's grounding influence, harmonizing with the Arcturian crystal's energy. These natural items serve as a link to the larger universe, grounding the space within the physical world while allowing it to remain open to the subtle energies of the crystal. Each natural element becomes a point of connection between the practitioner, the Earth, and the energy field they are creating, strengthening the foundation of the sacred space.

Regular maintenance of the sacred space ensures it remains energetically clear and aligned with the practitioner's intentions. Every week or month, practitioners return to cleanse the area again, perhaps adding a new element, adjusting the layout, or refreshing the crystal's energy by holding it, setting a renewed intention, and placing it back in its spot. These small acts of care and attention keep the space vibrant, a living environment that adapts to the practitioner's own growth and journey. Over time, the space evolves, becoming more than a corner or room—it transforms into a supportive presence, a place of quiet resilience and strength that reflects the practitioner's ongoing path.

Through the creation and care of this sacred space, practitioners establish a constant connection to the Arcturian crystal's energy. The space becomes a refuge where they can retreat, reflect, and reconnect whenever needed. The crystal, central to this sanctuary, provides a steady influence that grounds and amplifies their intentions, supporting the practitioner's peace and growth. This sacred space becomes an extension of the practitioner's spirit, a vessel that holds their dreams, goals, and sense of purpose.

In cultivating this area, practitioners create more than just a physical setting—they establish a personal sanctuary that fosters spiritual clarity, inner peace, and focused energy. This space, held by the Arcturian crystal, becomes an ever-present reminder of the practitioner's intentions, a place where they can access their higher self and return to center amidst the rhythms of daily life. Through this sacred space, they cultivate a deep sense of presence, a quiet strength that nurtures both the inner journey and the outer world.

With a sacred space established, practitioners can now explore advanced techniques to deepen its energy, transforming it into a powerful sanctuary for spiritual growth and personal alignment. By working with Arcturian crystals, they infuse the area with an energy that is both protective and expansive, creating a resonance that elevates their experiences within the space. This part of the journey delves into practices to enhance and refine the sacred space, focusing on rituals, altars, and energetic alignment that harmonize the crystal's frequency with the practitioner's intentions.

To begin deepening the energy of the sacred space, practitioners can create a central altar that serves as both a focal point and an energetic anchor. This altar may rest on a small table, shelf, or any dedicated surface within the space. Here, they arrange the Arcturian crystal as the centerpiece, representing a bridge between their inner self and the wider universe. Around it, they place items that embody their spiritual intentions, such as candles for clarity, incense for purification, or symbols of personal significance. Each item on the altar holds a purpose, reinforcing the space's energy and creating a layered resonance that supports meditation, reflection, and connection.

One technique for amplifying the crystal's presence within the sacred space is known as the "crystal grid." This involves placing several smaller crystals around the central Arcturian crystal in geometric formations. Practitioners might use a circle, triangle, or other shapes that resonate with them, arranging the crystals in a symmetrical pattern that enhances the flow of energy. Each crystal in the grid serves as a conduit, linking with the central crystal and spreading its frequency throughout the space. As the grid settles, it creates a cohesive field that radiates a sense of peace and stability, transforming the space into an environment that feels alive with supportive energy.

Once the altar and crystal grid are established, practitioners can use daily rituals to keep the sacred space energetically clear and aligned with their intentions. A simple yet powerful ritual involves lighting a candle each morning or evening, holding the Arcturian crystal in both hands, and taking a few moments to set a specific intention for the day. As the candle burns, the light serves as a reminder of this intention, a visible expression of the energy flowing within the space. Practitioners can sit in stillness, observing the candle's flame, allowing it to merge with the crystal's light, and feeling the space around them harmonize with their purpose.

To further infuse the space with presence, practitioners might experiment with sound, using bells, chimes, or singing bowls. Beginning at the altar, they gently ring the bell or chime, allowing the sound to resonate through the room, dissolving any stagnant energy. Moving around the space, they carry the sound to each corner, as if painting the air with intention, blending it with the crystal's energy. This practice purifies and refines the atmosphere, bringing a renewed vibrancy to the space, creating a sanctuary that feels deeply alive and connected to the crystal's protective and expansive qualities.

Practitioners can also work with the energy of the natural elements to enhance the sacred space. They may introduce a small water bowl, a symbol of flow and emotional balance, placing it on the altar near the Arcturian crystal. Alongside this, they might include a small plant or stone to represent grounding and life, and a feather or incense to embody air and inspiration. These natural elements harmonize with the crystal's energy, creating a balanced and holistic field within the sacred space. This grounding in nature serves as a reminder of the interconnectedness of life, strengthening the practitioner's bond with both Earth and spirit.

A powerful way to align with the crystal's frequency is through periodic "energy attunement" sessions within the space. During these sessions, practitioners sit in stillness before the altar, focusing their awareness on the crystal. They close their eyes, breathing in its energy, visualizing it as a soft light that fills the body with a sense of calm and presence. With each inhale, they draw the crystal's frequency into themselves, feeling it expand through the heart, the mind, and then out into the space. This visualization deepens the connection between the practitioner and the sacred space, creating a resonance that feels both personal and universal, an alignment with the Arcturian energy that the crystal holds.

Maintaining an intentional journal near the sacred space is another way to reinforce its energy. After each visit to the space or session with the crystal, practitioners can jot down any insights, thoughts, or impressions that arise. These reflections create a continuity, an unfolding record of their journey, one that adds a layer of personal energy to the space. Each journal entry reinforces the intention of the sacred space, making it a repository not only for items but for experiences, feelings, and growth.

Practitioners may also introduce guided visualizations within the sacred space, using the Arcturian crystal as a focal point for inner journeys. Sitting comfortably, they hold or place the crystal at the altar, closing their eyes and imagining the space around them filling with a soft, radiant light. In this visualization, they see themselves surrounded by an energy field that protects, nourishes, and guides them, allowing them to relax completely. They might visualize themselves moving deeper within this field, as though it is a cocoon of light, a space where they can safely explore their own spirit and intentions. This visualization strengthens the sacred space's protective nature, helping practitioners connect with their own essence while feeling supported by the crystal's energy.

Another powerful ritual for advanced practice involves periodic reactivation of the crystal's energy within the sacred space. Practitioners hold the Arcturian crystal, focusing on their intention for the space, and visualize the crystal absorbing this renewed purpose. They place it back on the altar with reverence, feeling as though they are recharging the space's energy, reinforcing it with each intention. This ritual keeps the space aligned with the practitioner's evolving spiritual journey, allowing it to remain dynamic and responsive to their inner growth.

As they work consistently with these practices, practitioners experience a deepening of their connection to the sacred space. It becomes more than a physical area; it is a realm of peace and clarity, an inner landscape reflected in the outer world. Through the presence of the Arcturian crystal, the space becomes a place of transformation, where the practitioner's intentions, dreams, and inner wisdom converge in harmony.

The sacred space, held and strengthened by the crystal, grows with the practitioner, adapting to their evolving path. It becomes a touchstone, a space they return to for grounding, inspiration, and spiritual nourishment. Through this space, practitioners develop a living relationship with the energy of the Arcturian crystal, discovering that their sanctuary is not only a place of stillness but also a space of active, vibrant transformation. As the sacred space matures, it becomes an unwavering presence in the practitioner's life, a sanctuary where the spirit finds both peace and the freedom to unfold, fully aligned with the quiet power and timeless energy of the crystal.

Chapter 19
Purification Rituals

Purification rituals are central to working with Arcturian crystals, as they cleanse both the physical and energetic realms, ensuring that the practitioner's personal field and environment stay in harmony. Through regular cleansing, practitioners release accumulated negativity and restore their connection to the crystal's frequency, allowing it to serve as a clear channel for Arcturian energy. Here, foundational purification rituals are introduced, each designed to maintain the vitality and clarity of the practitioner's aura, environment, and intentions.

A powerful starting ritual involves an "energetic bath" with the crystal, where practitioners combine the cleansing power of water with the crystal's purifying energy. They begin by preparing a bath or a bowl of water, optionally adding a few drops of lavender or rosemary essential oil, both known for their cleansing qualities. Holding the Arcturian crystal over the water, practitioners set an intention for the water to absorb the crystal's purifying light. They then lower the crystal into the water, visualizing the entire bowl or bath filling with light to create a pool of purity. As they wash their hands, face, or body with this water, they imagine any lingering negativity dissolving, replaced by the crystal's clear, calming energy. This ritual provides a full-body reset, refreshing the spirit and releasing stagnant energies.

Another effective technique for purification is "smudging," an ancient practice using the smoke of sacred plants to cleanse space and spirit. Practitioners choose sage, palo santo, or another cleansing herb, lighting it until it produces a steady smoke. They hold the Arcturian crystal in one hand and move the smoking herb around their body, envisioning the smoke lifting away any dense or heavy energy, leaving behind only clarity and light. As the smoke surrounds the crystal, it too becomes refreshed, recharged, and cleared, ready to resume its work with the practitioner. This practice is particularly powerful after emotional or stressful experiences, restoring the practitioner's sense of peace and balance.

Practitioners may also incorporate the element of sound into their purification rituals. Using a singing bowl, chime, or bell, they sound the instrument in a steady rhythm, allowing its resonance to cleanse both the crystal and the surrounding space. Starting with the crystal held in their hands, they gently tap or play the instrument, imagining the vibrations traveling through the crystal, dissolving any energy that no longer serves their purpose. As they continue, they move through their personal space, filling each corner with sound that clears, brightens, and rejuvenates the energy around them. This method is particularly effective when preparing the space for meditation or other focused work, ensuring that only the purest vibrations remain.

"Sun and moon charging" is a natural purification technique that works in harmony with the cosmic cycles. Practitioners place their Arcturian crystal outside or on a windowsill during the early morning hours or under the full moon, allowing it to absorb the balancing energies of the sun or moonlight. This practice not only purifies the crystal but also infuses it with powerful celestial energy. The sun charges the crystal with vitality and positivity, while the moon aligns it with gentle, introspective frequencies. As the light fills the crystal, practitioners feel a renewed connection to their intentions, sensing the alignment between their goals and the broader universe.

For personal purification, practitioners can engage in a focused breathing ritual with the Arcturian crystal. They sit in a comfortable space, holding the crystal in both hands and closing their eyes. Taking a deep breath in, they imagine that they are drawing light from the crystal directly into their heart, filling their entire body with each inhale. With every exhale, they release any tension or negative energy, feeling it dissolve into the air around them. This breathing practice connects their inner energy field to the crystal's frequency, creating a feedback loop of purity and harmony. This ritual not only clears their energy but also strengthens their alignment with the crystal, enhancing its effectiveness in future practices.

Another purification ritual involves creating a "crystal circle" around the practitioner, establishing a boundary of cleansing energy. Practitioners select several small stones or crystals, placing them in a circle around where they will sit or meditate, and holding the Arcturian crystal in their hands at the center of the circle. Once seated, they visualize the circle forming a protective boundary, a sacred space where only positive energy can enter. They breathe deeply, allowing the crystal's energy to extend outward until it fills the entire circle, establishing a field of calm clarity. This crystal circle not only purifies the practitioner's immediate space but also builds a secure boundary that strengthens their focus and peace.

To keep the environment continuously purified, practitioners may create a simple "blessing spray" with the Arcturian crystal's energy. In a small spray bottle, they combine water with a few drops of essential oil, like eucalyptus or frankincense, known for their purifying qualities. Holding the Arcturian crystal above the bottle, they set the intention for purity and peace, visualizing light from the crystal infusing the water. This spray becomes a mobile purification tool that practitioners can use to refresh their space, especially after interactions or activities that may have introduced heavy or distracting energy. A few spritzes clear the air, leaving the space energetically light and clear.

By integrating these purification rituals into their practice, practitioners cultivate a routine that keeps their energy field and environment balanced and receptive. With each cleansing, they create a space for clarity, a blank canvas upon which they can build their intentions, work, and personal growth. The Arcturian crystal, central to these rituals, serves as both a tool and a partner, its presence an anchor of purity and resilience.

In committing to these regular practices, practitioners maintain a clear pathway for their energy, unencumbered by negativity or past experiences. Each ritual becomes a moment of reconnection, an opportunity to release what no longer serves and invite a renewed sense of purpose. Through the purity of the crystal and the power of intention, practitioners foster a state of openness, a readiness to engage fully with their journey, knowing that their path remains aligned, clear, and energized.

Building on foundational purification practices, this phase delves into advanced rituals that unlock the full potential of Arcturian crystals for deep spiritual cleansing and alignment. These enhanced techniques involve layered energies, intricate visualizations, and ceremonial structures that empower practitioners to cleanse not only their personal energy but also their environment, relationships, and intentions. Through these practices, the Arcturian crystal serves as a guide in a comprehensive journey of renewal, supporting a holistic purification that touches every area of life.

One of the most potent advanced rituals is the *Ceremonial Aura Cleansing*, a process that infuses the crystal's energy into the practitioner's aura to create a protective shield that repels unwanted energies. Practitioners begin by finding a quiet, dimly lit space and lighting a candle as a symbol of illumination and clarity. Holding the Arcturian crystal, they close their eyes and focus on their breath, allowing the mind to clear. In their mind's eye, they visualize their aura as a soft light surrounding their body. With each breath, they see this light expand and brighten, filling any areas that feel heavy or dark. Gradually, they imagine the crystal's energy merging with their aura, weaving through it in a spiral motion, lifting away lingering negative energies and creating a field of purity. This practice not only cleanses but also fortifies the aura, establishing a protective boundary infused with the crystal's energy.

For practitioners wishing to cleanse an entire space, the Crystal Water Anointment ritual is a powerful method. They begin by filling a bowl with water, ideally purified or distilled, and placing the Arcturian crystal inside. Setting their intention for purification, they let the crystal sit in the water for several hours, absorbing the water's cleansing properties and infusing it with their purpose. Once ready, practitioners carefully remove the crystal and use the water to anoint doorways, windows, and corners of the space, imagining each drop of water as a spark of cleansing light. With each anointed area, they visualize the space becoming lighter, clearer, and aligned with peaceful energy. This ritual leaves a subtle yet lasting imprint, creating an environment that remains vibrantly positive.

Another advanced method, the Crystal Purification Grid, allows practitioners to create a dedicated space for ongoing purification. To construct this grid, they gather several smaller stones or crystals, positioning them in a circular or geometric arrangement around the Arcturian crystal. They might choose stones known for their cleansing properties, such as clear quartz or black tourmaline, to enhance the purifying effect. Once arranged, practitioners focus on the grid, visualizing light moving from the Arcturian crystal outward to each stone, weaving a network of energy that clears and protects. This grid can be left in place for continuous cleansing, serving as a source of calm and clarity for the space.

For personal purification on a soul level, the Guided Releasing Ceremony with the Arcturian crystal supports the practitioner in letting go of emotional or spiritual blockages. Sitting in a quiet space with the crystal held at the heart, practitioners allow memories, feelings, or patterns they wish to release to come to mind. As each memory or thought surfaces, they imagine it as a mist that rises from their heart and flows into the crystal, where it is purified and transformed. This visualization creates a sense of lightness, as though the crystal absorbs and refines each emotion, leaving only clarity and peace.

This ceremony becomes an intimate journey of letting go, one that fosters healing on a deeply personal level.

For a more structured and intensive ritual, practitioners may engage in the Crystal-Infused Smoke Purification Ceremony. Here, they prepare by placing the Arcturian crystal at the center of their sacred space and lighting incense or herbs with purifying properties, such as frankincense or juniper. Moving in a circle around the crystal, they waft the smoke in spirals, visualizing it carrying away residual energies from the space. With each movement, they imagine the smoke binding to negative energies, lifting them away and leaving the space crystal-clear. Afterward, they allow the smoke to settle around the crystal, which absorbs the purified energy, radiating it back into the space. This ceremonial approach imbues the area with a sense of reverence, creating a space that feels deeply sacred and protected.

Another advanced purification method is the Purpose Reinforcement Ritual, which cleanses and renews the practitioner's intentions with the crystal's energy. Practitioners sit in a dedicated space, holding the crystal while silently recalling their intentions or goals. As each intention rises, they imagine it as a thread of light moving from their heart into the crystal, where it is met with the crystal's energy. They visualize this meeting as a bright spark, a merging of their purpose with the crystal's pure frequency. This practice not only purifies the intentions, releasing any doubt or distraction, but also reinforces them, embedding each purpose within the crystal's energy. This ritual leaves the practitioner with a sense of clarity, a feeling that their intentions are aligned and supported.

To maintain the crystal's own purity, practitioners can engage in the Earth Recharging Ritual, a grounding method that uses the natural cleansing power of the Earth. Practitioners find a quiet outdoor space and gently bury the Arcturian crystal in the soil, setting the intention for renewal. They leave it buried overnight or for a full day, allowing the Earth's energy to cleanse and recharge the crystal. When they retrieve the crystal, they sense its renewed vitality, as though it has been washed in natural purity. This practice connects the crystal to the Earth's grounding energy, strengthening its purity and enhancing its resonance with the practitioner's intentions.

The Full-Moon Purification Ceremony offers a chance to purify and recharge both the crystal and the practitioner's intentions under the moon's reflective light. Practitioners place the Arcturian crystal under the open sky on the night of a full moon, allowing it to absorb the moonlight. They sit nearby, reflecting on what they wish to release and what they intend to invite into their lives. As the crystal absorbs the moon's energy, practitioners focus on their intentions, feeling as though the light amplifies and clarifies each one. Afterward, the crystal is charged with both the purity of the moon and the strength of the practitioner's purpose, ready to support the journey forward.

These advanced purification rituals serve as touchstones on the practitioner's path, providing moments of renewal, release, and reconnection. Through them, the Arcturian crystal transforms into a steadfast ally in the journey of spiritual and personal evolution. With each ritual, practitioners not only cleanse their energy but align more closely with their intentions, cultivating a path that feels both grounded and expansive, rooted in clarity and purpose.

Chapter 20
Strengthening the Energetic Field

Strengthening the energetic field is a practice that extends beyond protection, connecting practitioners to their inner resilience and fostering an energetic presence that is both grounded and expansive. With Arcturian crystals, fortifying the energetic field becomes an art—balancing personal power with alignment to universal energy. This phase introduces essential techniques to reinforce the energetic field, enabling practitioners to engage with life from a place of inner strength and clarity. Through these practices, the Arcturian crystal serves as an anchor, supporting a steady and vibrant energy field that harmonizes with the practitioner's purpose and well-being.

One of the most direct methods for strengthening the energetic field involves breathwork with the Arcturian crystal, using breath to circulate and expand the practitioner's energy. Sitting comfortably, practitioners hold the Arcturian crystal at their heart and close their eyes. They take a slow, deep breath, visualizing light from the crystal entering with each inhale, traveling through the body, and radiating outward in all directions. Each exhale releases tension, refining the energy field layer by layer. After several cycles, the practitioner envisions their energy field as a glowing sphere around them—bright, resilient, and held in place by the steady rhythm of their breath. This practice builds a powerful energetic foundation, a balanced field that remains clear and strong, enhancing the practitioner's sense of personal presence.

For practitioners who wish to establish a deeper connection with the Arcturian crystal, hand placements serve as an accessible yet profound technique. Sitting quietly, they place the crystal in one hand, and with the other hand, gently touch areas associated with energy centers, such as the heart or solar plexus. As they do, they envision the crystal's energy flowing into the chosen center, creating a link between their body's energy and the crystal's frequency. Moving slowly, they sense the energy spreading, each touch infusing them with a stabilizing presence. This tactile connection grounds the practitioner's energy field, reinforcing it with the crystal's qualities of balance, protection, and calm. Each touch serves as a reminder of their energetic boundaries and the resilience embedded within them.

Another powerful method involves visualization to expand the energetic field using the crystal as a focal point. Practitioners hold the crystal and close their eyes, imagining a radiant sphere of energy surrounding their body. In this sphere, they envision colors that represent strength and tranquility—perhaps a deep blue for calm or a shimmering gold for protection. Holding these colors in mind, they visualize the sphere growing brighter and more defined, solidifying the boundaries around them. With the Arcturian crystal amplifying their focus, they allow this energy to expand, forming a field that remains present and vibrant, even after the visualization ends. This technique helps practitioners maintain a strengthened, flexible boundary, one that adapts to life's fluctuations while holding steady.

To further enhance this practice, practitioners can engage in a standing grounding ritual with the Arcturian crystal. Standing barefoot if possible, they hold the crystal close to their center, focusing on the connection between their feet and the ground. They imagine roots growing from their feet into the Earth, a grounding connection that stabilizes their entire being. As they breathe, they feel energy rising from the Earth into their body, flowing through them and merging with the crystal's frequency. With each breath, the energy field strengthens, creating a harmonious balance between groundedness and elevated energy.

This standing ritual is particularly effective in moments of transition or before engaging in activities that require focus and endurance, as it connects practitioners to both the Earth and the crystal's stabilizing energy.

The mirror technique offers a unique approach to visualizing and reinforcing the energetic field. Practitioners stand before a mirror, holding the Arcturian crystal at their heart, and look into their own eyes, visualizing their energy field reflected back to them. They imagine this field as a luminous aura that radiates outward, expanding as they focus. In the mirror, they see not just themselves, but the field of energy they are cultivating. This image imprints a sense of strength and presence, reinforcing the idea that their field is a living, dynamic boundary. This technique empowers the practitioner's self-perception, reinforcing their energetic resilience each time they see their reflection.

For moments of heightened stress or energy drain, the palm press technique helps to quickly reinforce the energetic field. Holding the Arcturian crystal between both palms, practitioners press their hands together at the heart or center of the chest, creating gentle pressure. They take several deep breaths, feeling the crystal's energy merging with their own. As they exhale, they sense this combined energy expanding outward, filling the space around them with warmth and strength. This quick but effective technique is a reminder of the body's power to support and reinforce itself, particularly when guided by the crystal's frequency. It serves as a grounding ritual that practitioners can use as a daily recharge or whenever they feel their energy waning.

Integrating intentional affirmations with the crystal further fortifies the practitioner's energy field. Sitting with the Arcturian crystal, they repeat simple, clear affirmations such as, "My energy is strong and protected," or "I am centered, calm, and resilient." Each affirmation becomes a thread in the fabric of their energy field, woven in with the crystal's vibration. They speak these words softly, visualizing them as beams of light that extend into the energy field, solidifying it and imbuing it with strength. This practice not only strengthens the field but also aligns it with the practitioner's intentions, creating a layer of energy that reflects their inner stability and confidence.

A field harmonization exercise with nature enhances the connection between the practitioner's energy field and the wider environment. Holding the Arcturian crystal, they spend time outdoors, perhaps sitting beneath a tree or near flowing water. As they tune into the natural world, they feel their energy field merging gently with the rhythms around them. With each breath, they allow their energy to sync with the sounds of nature—the wind, the rustling leaves, or the flow of water. This harmonization expands the energy field, creating a resonance with the Earth itself. In these moments, the Arcturian crystal serves as a bridge, connecting their personal energy to the boundless support of nature, leaving them with a field that is not only strong but attuned to the natural flow of life.

Through these practices, practitioners not only strengthen their energetic field but cultivate a steady, responsive presence that aligns with their highest intentions. As the Arcturian crystal amplifies and grounds their energy, the field becomes a source of personal power, one that supports every interaction, experience, and choice.

o fully cultivate a fortified energetic field, practitioners benefit from advanced practices that synchronize their personal energy with Arcturian frequencies at a profound level. This stage introduces refined methods to strengthen the energetic field with the Arcturian crystal, emphasizing complex breathwork, layered visualizations, and alignment with universal energies. Each technique builds upon foundational practices, guiding practitioners to reach new depths of energetic resilience and connection, enabling them to remain grounded, adaptable, and aligned with their highest purpose.

Through these advanced practices, the Arcturian crystal supports a dynamic energetic field that not only protects but also nourishes, connecting practitioners deeply with their inner strength and the expansive, harmonious flow of universal energy.

A highly focused method is the Three-Breath Energy Infusion, where practitioners harness the power of breath in distinct stages, using the Arcturian crystal as a guide. Sitting with the crystal held near the heart, practitioners take their first deep breath, visualizing energy from the crystal moving into their body. They hold this energy momentarily, letting it settle within their core. On the second breath, they visualize this energy spreading, filling every corner of their body.

With the third breath, they see the energy expanding beyond the physical form, forming a protective yet flexible boundary around them. This three-breath technique empowers practitioners with a reinforced energetic field that remains vibrant, a field that breathes and moves with them as they navigate their day.

For those seeking to establish a harmonious balance between grounding and expansion, the Root and Crown Circuit technique integrates both Earth and cosmic energy. Practitioners sit with the Arcturian crystal in one hand and place the other hand palm-down toward the Earth, either resting on the ground or symbolically connecting to it. They close their eyes and visualize a thread of energy extending from the crystal down into the Earth, rooting deeply, drawing stability, and grounding. Simultaneously, they imagine another thread of light extending upward from the crown of their head, connecting to the Arcturian frequency in the cosmos. These two currents, Earth and cosmic energy, merge within the practitioner's heart, where the Arcturian crystal rests, creating a strong, balanced field that connects them to both the physical and the spiritual. This dual connection results in a field that feels grounded yet expansive, firmly anchored yet open to higher insights.

The Aura Weaving Practice is an advanced technique that further solidifies the energetic field by "weaving" layers of light through the practitioner's aura. Holding the Arcturian crystal, practitioners visualize soft strands of light extending from the crystal and weaving through the energy field around them. Each strand represents a quality they wish to reinforce—perhaps peace, strength, or clarity. They envision these strands intersecting, creating a tapestry of energy that strengthens and aligns their field. This woven structure becomes a dynamic shield, one that moves and adapts, filtering out external disruptions while retaining the core energies of the practitioner. This practice reinforces their sense of self within the energetic field, allowing it to serve as a barrier and a source of calm, inner stability.

Another powerful technique, the Directional Field Charging, uses specific body movements to channel and concentrate the crystal's energy into the field. Standing with the Arcturian crystal held close to their heart, practitioners slowly extend one arm forward, visualizing energy radiating outward from the crystal through their extended hand. They turn in a full circle, consciously infusing their energy field with the crystal's frequency as they move. This rotation expands the energy evenly in all directions, creating a balanced, 360-degree shield. Each turn reinforces the boundaries, creating a unified field that surrounds them in a stable sphere of the Arcturian energy. This technique is particularly effective before entering crowded or intense environments, where energetic stability and clarity are essential.

For those who feel ready to deepen their connection with the Arcturian crystal, the Inner Sanctum Meditation offers a way to cultivate an intimate bond with the crystal's energy, strengthening the field from the inside out. Practitioners close their eyes and visualize themselves entering an inner chamber within their heart space, a peaceful sanctuary where the crystal's energy resides. In this visualization, they see themselves holding the crystal, feeling its vibration resonate with their entire being. The energy expands, filling every corner of this inner sanctum, then radiates outward, expanding through the body and into the field. This inner journey not only reinforces their energetic boundaries but also fortifies the connection between their own essence and the Arcturian frequency, creating a field that reflects their deepest intentions and aligns with their true self.

Crystal Alignment Breathing is another advanced practice designed to attune the energy field to the crystal's frequency.

Practitioners lie down with the Arcturian crystal placed on their solar plexus or heart, closing their eyes and focusing on their breath. With each inhale, they visualize the crystal's energy flowing through the body in a wave, expanding outwards until it fills the energy field. With each exhale, they feel the energy settling, rooting, and becoming part of their own frequency. As the breathing continues, the field grows stronger and more defined, the crystal's vibration harmonizing with the practitioner's energy, creating a field that resonates with calm power.

A unique approach to strengthening the field is the Light Pillar Visualization, a technique that connects the practitioner to both Earth and cosmic energies through the Arcturian crystal. Holding the crystal close, practitioners imagine a pillar of light descending from the sky, passing through the crystal and grounding deep into the Earth below. This pillar becomes a stabilizing force, connecting all layers of their energy field to both cosmic and earthly energies. As they hold this visualization, they feel a sense of weight and lightness, as though they are both anchored and expanded. The light pillar enhances their energetic resilience, creating a sense of balance and fortification that supports them in any situation.

The Field Resonance Activation technique allows practitioners to amplify the vibration of their energy field, creating a resonance that remains active and protective throughout the day. Practitioners hold the crystal and imagine it as a tuning fork, gently vibrating, sending ripples of energy through their field. They visualize these vibrations as concentric waves, each wave strengthening their field and attuning it to the crystal's high frequency. This field resonance creates a buffer that filters out disruptive energies, leaving only what is aligned with the practitioner's intentions. As they complete this practice, they feel surrounded by an energy that is harmonized, expansive, and uniquely their own, a field that resonates with their true essence.

Each of these advanced techniques builds upon the foundational practices, offering deeper levels of energetic alignment and resilience. By working closely with the Arcturian crystal, practitioners cultivate a field that is both a boundary and a bridge, a reflection of their inner harmony and connection to universal energies. Through these practices, they develop an energetic presence that not only supports their journey but enhances it, creating a state of balance that resonates from within.

Chapter 21
Energizing Crystals

Energizing crystals is a practice that infuses them with renewed vitality, aligning them with both the practitioner's intentions and the Arcturian frequency. Through this, the crystal transforms into a powerful source of strength, protection, and clarity, prepared to support a variety of energetic and spiritual practices. Here, foundational techniques to energize Arcturian crystals are introduced, guiding practitioners through processes that deepen their bond with the crystal and its purpose. Through these methods, the crystal becomes more than a tool—it becomes an active participant in the practitioner's journey, radiating with life and intent.

One of the most accessible ways to energize an Arcturian crystal is through Solar and Lunar Charging, which utilizes the transformative energies of sunlight and moonlight. Practitioners begin by placing the crystal where it will be exposed to either morning sunlight or the light of a full moon. With the crystal positioned, they close their eyes and set an intention, visualizing the light infusing the crystal with pure energy. Sunlight charges the crystal with warmth, optimism, and vitality, ideal for grounding and empowerment. Moonlight, with its cooler, more reflective energy, aligns the crystal with intuition, mystery, and spiritual insight. By selecting the appropriate light source, practitioners energize the crystal with a frequency that matches their needs, creating a radiant source of energy that mirrors the natural cycles.

A deeply personal technique involves Breath Energizing, which infuses the crystal with the practitioner's own life force. Holding the Arcturian crystal close to their heart, practitioners take a series of deep breaths, focusing on their own energy as it flows through their body. With each exhale, they direct a breath toward the crystal, imagining their intention or energy as a radiant light entering the stone. This breathing technique creates a unique bond between the practitioner and the crystal, allowing the crystal to resonate with the practitioner's specific energetic signature. Each breath strengthens this connection, creating an energized crystal that is attuned to the individual's frequency, ready to work in harmony with their goals and intentions.

Hand Placement Energizing is a grounding technique that draws on the practitioner's natural energy field. Sitting comfortably, practitioners hold the Arcturian crystal in one hand, placing their other hand over it. They close their eyes and envision a stream of energy moving from their heart, through their hands, and into the crystal. With each pulse of energy, they imagine the crystal growing brighter, its power expanding with every touch. This technique fosters a direct, tactile connection to the crystal, reinforcing it with the practitioner's own life force while grounding its energy in the physical realm. This practice can be repeated frequently, allowing the crystal to stay consistently energized and closely attuned to the practitioner's presence.

For those who prefer a more elemental approach, the Water and Earth Charging technique offers a way to ground the crystal in natural energies. Practitioners fill a small bowl with water, ideally sourced from a natural spring or distilled, and place the crystal within. They set an intention for purity and renewal, allowing the water's cleansing properties to wash over the crystal. Once the water ritual is complete, the crystal can be briefly buried in soil, either outdoors or within a pot, symbolizing a reconnection to Earth. These elements—water and earth—imbue the crystal with balance, grounding, and natural vitality, creating a well-rounded energy that is both soothing and stabilizing.

Another highly effective method is Resonant Sound Energizing, which uses sound to awaken and activate the crystal's inherent energies. Practitioners may use a singing bowl, bell, or chime, creating a rhythmic sound that envelops the crystal. As the sound waves move through the crystal, practitioners visualize the vibrations breaking up any stagnant or dormant energy, leaving behind a field of clarity and vibrancy. Each sound reinforces the crystal's energy, aligning it with the resonance of the practitioner's intention. This technique is particularly beneficial for clearing and re-energizing a crystal that has absorbed heavy or dense energies, as it restores the stone's natural frequency, preparing it for renewed use.

Crystal Gridding for Energizing is an advanced method that involves creating a geometric arrangement with the Arcturian crystal at its center. Practitioners select other stones or crystals that resonate with their intention, such as clear quartz for amplification or amethyst for spiritual connection. Arranging these stones in a circle or other sacred shape, they place the Arcturian crystal in the middle, envisioning energy moving between each stone, converging at the center. This grid acts as a conduit, drawing in energies from all directions and focusing them within the Arcturian crystal. This technique creates a powerful concentration of energy, a field that can be used to amplify the crystal's power for healing, protection, or manifestation.

For a more introspective approach, the Intentional Meditation Energizing method allows practitioners to enter a state of deep concentration, infusing the crystal with focused purpose. Holding the Arcturian crystal, they close their eyes and visualize a specific intention—a purpose or quality they wish the crystal to embody. As they breathe, they imagine this intention as a glowing light, growing stronger with each heartbeat and breath. They then see this light entering the crystal, merging with it, and radiating outward. This practice not only energizes the crystal but also imbues it with a clear, purposeful direction, aligning it with the practitioner's path.

Physical Movement Energizing is a dynamic technique that channels kinetic energy into the Arcturian crystal, ideal for practitioners who feel connected to their bodies. Holding the crystal, they engage in gentle movement, such as walking, dancing, or stretching, feeling their body's natural energy flow as it moves through the crystal. This motion becomes a source of power, with each step or sway infusing the crystal with the practitioner's vitality and focus. This method grounds the crystal's energy in the present moment, enhancing its power with the immediacy and clarity that movement brings.

Visualization Infusion invites practitioners to strengthen their connection to the crystal through imagery and imagination. In a quiet space, they close their eyes and hold the Arcturian crystal, visualizing it as a small sun, glowing with vibrant energy. They picture light flowing into it from above, a limitless stream of pure energy filling the crystal. As the light intensifies, they feel it radiate through their hands and into their own field, forming a circuit of energy that flows continuously between them and the crystal. This visualization not only energizes the crystal but also creates an enduring bond, linking the practitioner's field with the Arcturian frequency.

Through these practices, the Arcturian crystal becomes more than a tool; it transforms into an active, responsive source of energy, reflecting the practitioner's intentions and resonating with their frequency. Each technique invites the practitioner into a deeper relationship with the crystal, creating a harmonious bond that empowers every future use. Energized and attuned, the crystal becomes a potent ally, ready to support, protect, and inspire the practitioner on their path.

With foundational energizing practices in place, practitioners can now explore advanced methods to charge Arcturian crystals. These refined techniques deepen the connection between the practitioner and the crystal, aligning it intricately with the Arcturian frequency. Through these advanced practices, the crystal becomes highly attuned, resonating not only with the practitioner's intentions but also with broader cosmic energies, forming a bridge between realms.

A powerful technique to begin with is *Cosmic Channeling*, an energizing ritual that channels energy directly from the cosmos to amplify the crystal's vibrational alignment. Practitioners hold the Arcturian crystal, visualizing themselves under an open night sky, with a vast field of stars above. In their mind's eye, they envision a column of starlight descending, connecting to the crystal. This light carries ancient wisdom and high-frequency Arcturian energy, infusing the crystal with celestial strength. As the energy flows through it, the crystal radiates a soft glow, embodying this universal connection. This technique aligns the crystal with cosmic energies, preparing it for enhanced healing, protection, and spiritual exploration.

For those seeking to tune the crystal's frequency specifically to the Arcturian vibration, Arcturian Invocation is an essential practice. In a quiet space, practitioners place the crystal in front of them, close their eyes, and silently invite the presence of Arcturian energies. Using a mantra or phrase that feels intuitively connected, they repeat it softly, feeling their words infuse the space around the crystal. They envision the crystal responding, its energy aligning with the unique, subtle frequency of Arcturian guidance and wisdom. This process may be repeated over multiple sessions, gradually refining the crystal's energetic structure to more clearly channel the Arcturian essence.

Another deepening method is Multi-Layered Visualization, which enhances the crystal's power by layering intentions into its energetic field. Holding the Arcturian crystal, practitioners visualize a sequence of energies entering it, each with a distinct quality they seek to embody—peace, clarity, strength, or protection. With each layer, they see the crystal becoming denser with purpose, its energy growing more complex and profound. This visualization turns the crystal into a multi-dimensional reservoir, prepared to support various practices by holding and transmitting a combination of qualities attuned to the practitioner's needs.

For those drawn to elemental energies, Fire and Smoke Energizing offers a path to revitalizing the crystal with transformative force. Practitioners begin by safely lighting a small candle and allowing the crystal to bask in its warmth, visualizing the flame purifying and igniting the crystal's energy. Then, using incense or a cleansing herb, they waft the smoke around the crystal, envisioning it absorbing the power of fire and air. This dual approach instills the crystal with both the clarity of fire and the freedom of air, qualities that prepare it for practices where dynamic energy and adaptability are needed.

Chakra Alignment Charging is an advanced practice that synchronizes the crystal with the practitioner's own chakra system, allowing the crystal to work more intimately with their energy centers. Practitioners lie down with the Arcturian crystal placed on each chakra in sequence, beginning with the root and moving upward. As the crystal rests on each chakra, they visualize energy flowing from that center into the crystal and vice versa, creating a two-way flow that balances both energies. This technique aligns the crystal to the body's own rhythms, attuning it to the practitioner's unique energetic signature. After this practice, the crystal becomes a personal ally, aligned to support chakra-based work and personal transformation.

In moments when practitioners need a high-intensity recharge, the Crystalline Light Amplification ritual allows them to magnify the crystal's energy field. They sit in a darkened room, holding the crystal at eye level, and light a small lamp or candle directly behind it. The light refracts through the crystal, illuminating its facets and energizing it with amplified light. They visualize this light as waves emanating from the crystal, filling the space around them with radiant energy. As the crystal absorbs this intensified light, it becomes charged with clarity and focus, ready for deep meditation or ritual work that requires heightened awareness and purity.

For an ongoing source of power, Continuous Charging Grids can be established to provide a stable stream of energy to the Arcturian crystal. Practitioners arrange smaller stones or symbols in a geometric pattern around the crystal, setting an intention for the grid to serve as a perpetual energy source. They periodically reinforce the grid by visualizing light moving from the outer stones to the center crystal, keeping the energy active and flowing. This grid maintains the crystal's vibrancy, allowing it to remain perpetually energized and ready for spontaneous use or long-term projects.

The Sacred Chant Charging technique draws on the power of sound to elevate the crystal's energy. Practitioners hold the Arcturian crystal while chanting a sacred mantra or sound, such as "Om" or another resonance that feels aligned with their purpose. They feel the vibrations of their voice permeate the crystal, leaving traces of sound within it, as though each syllable carves an energetic groove into its structure. The sound frequencies expand the crystal's capacity, enabling it to resonate more deeply with universal energies. This method is especially effective for preparing the crystal for spiritual or ceremonial work, where an amplified, refined energy is essential.

For practitioners wishing to deepen their energetic connection, Heartbeat Synchronization offers a way to blend the rhythm of their own pulse with the crystal's energy. Holding the crystal over the heart, they close their eyes and listen to the beat of their heart, allowing this natural rhythm to sync with the crystal. As they breathe, they feel the heartbeat moving into the crystal, infusing it with a uniquely personal vibration. This intimate bond creates a crystal that resonates with the practitioner's physical essence, prepared to serve as a grounding and supportive force in their everyday life.

Divine Alignment Meditation is a profound technique for connecting the Arcturian crystal with energies beyond the physical realm, an energizing practice that aligns the crystal with universal wisdom and guidance. In a meditative state, practitioners visualize their connection to higher energies—whatever they feel drawn to, whether that be the Arcturian frequency, angelic realms, or cosmic consciousness. They hold the crystal as a bridge, imagining these elevated energies entering it, charging it with layers of wisdom and insight that transcend ordinary experience. This method leaves the crystal in a state of heightened readiness, open to channel spiritual messages and intuitive insights for the practitioner.

Through these refined practices, the Arcturian crystal is transformed into a charged, multi-layered source of power, deeply attuned to cosmic and personal energies alike. Each technique shapes it into a purposeful vessel, resonant with higher frequencies and prepared to serve as a powerful companion on the practitioner's path. With this energized connection, the crystal becomes a gateway to enhanced experiences, its energy alive, responsive, and ready to support the practitioner's deepest intentions.

Chapter 22
Protection Against Negative Energies

The Arcturian crystals hold a powerful capacity to shield practitioners from negative energies, forming an energetic barrier against unwanted influences. Their resonance can ward off dense or harmful vibrations, making these crystals potent protectors for environments, personal space, and spiritual well-being. Working with these crystals allows one to create a sanctuary of light, a field of harmonious energy that acts as a shield against lower frequencies.

The process of creating this protection begins with understanding the nature of energetic boundaries. Negative energies are often subtle, entering through stress, unresolved emotions, or even proximity to charged environments. When working with Arcturian crystals for protection, practitioners first need to align with a clear intent, visualizing the crystal as an energetic guard. Holding the crystal, they can breathe deeply, grounding themselves, and feeling the crystal's energy merge with their own. As they establish this connection, they envision a soft, luminous barrier forming around them—a protective cocoon that only allows in light and positivity.

One fundamental method to work with these crystals for protection is through Warding Visualization. Here, the practitioner holds the crystal and visualizes a radiant shield enveloping their body, starting from the heart and expanding outward. This shield, infused with the energy of the Arcturian crystal, acts like a force field, repelling all unwanted energies. As they breathe deeply, they visualize this field becoming stronger, brighter, and more impenetrable. Each breath reinforces the shield, building layers of protection that last beyond the meditation itself.

For practitioners desiring a more tangible approach, Crystal Carrying for Continuous Protection offers a steady defense. By carrying an Arcturian crystal in a pocket, wearing it as jewelry, or placing it near their workspace, practitioners create a consistent source of shielding energy. Throughout the day, they can touch or hold the crystal briefly, reaffirming its purpose as a protective ally. Each time they do this, they are reminded of the crystal's presence, keeping their mind attuned to the protective barrier it provides, grounding them in an awareness of their protected state.

Energy Cleansing with Protective Intention is another essential technique for practitioners aiming to shield themselves from negative energies. By gently rubbing the Arcturian crystal along their body, starting at the top of the head and moving down to the feet, they use the stone to sweep away any accumulated energy that feels heavy or stagnant. As they perform this cleansing, they visualize the crystal absorbing and neutralizing negative energies, which are then released harmlessly into the earth. This process can be used at the end of a day or after a period spent in a high-energy environment, keeping the practitioner's energetic field clear and balanced.

For a stronger form of protection, practitioners can explore Energetic Sealing with the Arcturian crystal. They begin by holding the crystal over their heart and setting an intention to seal their aura from any external influences. Envisioning the crystal's energy merging with their own, they mentally guide this combined energy through their entire aura, starting from the center and expanding outward to create a seamless, impermeable layer. This technique is particularly useful before entering crowded spaces, as it seals their energy from others, keeping them grounded and centered in their own essence.

When protecting physical spaces, Placement Grids are a powerful method to shield an environment. Practitioners place

Arcturian crystals at the four corners of a room, or around a space they wish to protect, creating a grid that amplifies and distributes the protective energy. They set an intention as they place each crystal, envisioning the grid forming a barrier around the space. This grid can remain in place permanently, with practitioners periodically recharging the crystals by holding them, visualizing renewed protective energy flowing into each point. In doing so, they create a lasting sanctuary, a protected environment where negativity cannot enter.

An enhanced method, Mirror Reflection Visualization, pairs with the Arcturian crystal to deflect negative energies back to their source without harm. Practitioners sit quietly with the crystal and visualize a mirrored sphere surrounding them, reflecting any incoming negativity back outwards. Holding the crystal, they imagine it strengthening this mirror, making it unbreakable and polished, sending away any harmful intent or energy. This reflective shield is particularly effective for encounters with challenging individuals or in high-energy situations, as it prevents the practitioner from absorbing any negativity directed their way.

Crystal Empowerment Affirmations allow practitioners to reinforce the protective role of the Arcturian crystal with words. Holding the crystal, they speak affirmations aloud, such as "This crystal shields me from all harm," "I am protected in all spaces," or "Only positive energy may enter my field." Each affirmation, spoken with intention, solidifies the crystal's role as a guardian. Repeating these words anchors the crystal's energy, merging verbal intent with the crystal's natural frequency, amplifying its power to guard and protect.

Through these practices, the Arcturian crystal becomes a shield of light and a guardian presence. Working with these techniques regularly, practitioners establish a steady, lasting field of protection that not only preserves their personal energy but also cultivates an environment of peace and positivity around them.

With the foundation of basic protection in place, practitioners can now explore advanced techniques that enhance the protective capabilities of Arcturian crystals. These methods go beyond shielding, actively repelling negative energies from both personal and external environments to create resilient fields of light. Practitioners can customize and reinforce this protective energy, making the crystal an adaptable, dynamic guardian that responds to shifting energetic needs and circumstances.

The first advanced technique, *Dynamic Energy Shielding*, involves the practitioner visualizing the protective energy around them as a living, breathing presence. Holding the Arcturian crystal, they picture an energetic shield that pulses and adjusts its intensity based on the surrounding environment. When sensing incoming negativity, the shield intensifies and solidifies, forming a bright, impermeable barrier. This visualization allows the shield to respond automatically to varying energy levels, providing heightened, adaptable protection. Practitioners reinforce this dynamic shield by spending a few minutes daily holding the crystal and setting a clear intention for protection, thereby strengthening the shield's responsiveness to energy shifts in their environment.

For those facing significant emotional or energetic turbulence, Protective Layering offers a way to fortify their shield further. Practitioners visualize their protective field as composed of multiple layers, each with a unique quality—strength, calmness, resilience. They hold the Arcturian crystal close and breathe deeply, imagining each breath adding a new layer to the shield. As they build these layers, they set an intention for each one, such as "This layer repels fear," or "This layer maintains my inner peace." With each added layer, the shield becomes increasingly resilient, allowing it to withstand multiple forms of external negativity while maintaining internal balance and harmony.

Deflective Energy Mirror is a method that allows practitioners to not only repel but also return energies to their origin point, ensuring their space remains undisturbed by external forces. They visualize the Arcturian crystal enveloping them in a mirrored sphere, reflective on the outside. Any negative energy directed toward them or their space is immediately reflected back, neutralized by the crystal's frequency. Practitioners reinforce this shield by holding the crystal, focusing on its reflective qualities, and visualizing the mirrored barrier surrounding them. This technique is especially valuable in situations where they encounter dense or chaotic environments, as it allows them to remain within a tranquil bubble, untouched by external interference.

Another potent technique for enhanced protection is Pulse Repulsion, where practitioners visualize their protective field expanding and contracting in powerful pulses. Holding the Arcturian crystal in one hand, they imagine it charging their field with waves of energy that push outward, creating a steady pulsing effect. This rhythmic pulsing forms a barrier that forcefully repels any energy that tries to penetrate it, sending it back with gentle but firm resistance. Practitioners can engage in this exercise before entering high-stress spaces, or whenever they feel the need for additional support, feeling the energy radiate outward in pulses that leave their field clear and defended.

For a shield that sustains itself over time, Crystal Grid Reinforcement provides a structured way to extend the crystal's protective energy to a larger area. Practitioners place several Arcturian crystals in a grid pattern around a designated space, creating a continuous line of protective energy that wraps around the environment. With a central crystal as the grid's focal point, they set an intention for long-lasting protection, visualizing a sphere of light expanding from the center and enveloping the entire space. By periodically charging each crystal with intent, practitioners can maintain a lasting energetic barrier, effectively creating a haven within which they can relax, meditate, or work in uninterrupted peace.

An approach that blends intention with physicality is Earthing Integration, which grounds the Arcturian crystal's energy into the earth itself to form a protective channel. Practitioners place the crystal on the ground, ideally in direct contact with natural earth, and hold their hands over it, channeling their intention for grounding and protection. They visualize a line of energy moving from the crystal down into the earth, creating an anchored connection. This technique allows them to draw on the grounding strength of the earth, creating a shield that feels rooted, unyielding, and deeply stable. As the earth absorbs and diffuses any incoming negativity, the practitioner remains insulated within a field that naturally cycles and releases disruptive energies.

To further amplify the Arcturian crystal's protective resonance, practitioners can engage in Channeled Light Invocation. Holding the crystal in both hands, they meditate on a connection to higher frequencies, envisioning a pure light descending and entering the crystal. This light becomes part of the crystal's structure, filling it with a radiant energy that enhances its shielding properties. They then visualize this light expanding outwards, covering them in a layer of high-frequency protection. This approach brings forth an additional layer of spiritual security, as it aligns the crystal with energies that resonate above and beyond earthly influences, creating a sense of calm that transcends daily disturbances.

Heartbeat Synchronization, another subtle but profound practice, allows practitioners to integrate the crystal's protective qualities with their own energy rhythms. They hold the crystal over their heart, close their eyes, and attune to the beat of their own pulse, feeling the crystal pulse in rhythm. As their heartbeat synchronizes with the crystal's energy, they visualize each beat sending out waves of protection, surrounding them with a barrier that is both deeply personal and robust. This technique makes the crystal's protection feel innate and inseparable from the practitioner's own energy, creating a continuous, unwavering shield.

For protection that aligns with cosmic and elemental forces, practitioners can engage in Celestial Charging, a technique that utilizes the light of the moon or sun. They place the Arcturian crystal under natural moonlight or sunlight, allowing it to absorb the pure energy of the cosmos. As it charges, they meditate on the crystal's role as a protective guardian, envisioning it radiating a strengthened field. This process heightens the crystal's natural protective capacity, creating a blend of celestial and earthly energies that forms a potent shield around both the practitioner and their space.

These advanced protective techniques deepen the Arcturian crystal's function as a guardian of personal energy, creating layers of defense that are both adaptive and enduring. Practitioners learn to work in harmony with the crystal, tapping into its potential to shield, reflect, and transform energies. Each method strengthens not only their energetic field but also their own awareness of the crystal's vast capabilities, making it a constant, empowered ally in their journey through both the visible and unseen worlds.

Chapter 23
Moments of Transition and Change

In life's moments of transition—those times of change that sweep us into the unknown and unfamiliar—the Arcturian crystals emerge as steadfast allies, radiating energy that guides, grounds, and strengthens. These moments of transformation may come in many forms: a new phase in life, a shift in relationships, changes in personal goals, or even times of emotional upheaval. The Arcturian crystals resonate with a frequency that is particularly stabilizing during these phases, providing a beacon of support when the path forward seems unclear.

Transitions often stir energies deep within, as we release what is no longer in harmony and make room for new possibilities. This process can bring to the surface unresolved feelings, old habits, and emotional patterns that need clearing. To aid in this release, practitioners can work with the Energetic Reset Ritual. In this practice, they hold an Arcturian crystal, visualizing it absorbing any lingering attachments to the past, unhealthy energies, or thoughts that no longer serve them. As they breathe out, they imagine the crystal drawing out these energies and dispersing them safely, leaving a feeling of lightness, clarity, and readiness for what lies ahead. With each exhalation, they envision themselves stepping into the new, untethered by the old.

For transitions that come with the unknown, when feelings of insecurity or doubt may arise, the Stabilizing Ground technique helps practitioners find a sense of steady footing. Sitting quietly with the crystal, they place it over their heart, feeling its energy align with their own. They take a deep breath, allowing the crystal's grounding energy to flow through them. In this state of calm, they visualize themselves as a tree with deep roots, unwavering even in strong winds. The crystal amplifies this grounded feeling, anchoring them so they can move forward with a sense of inner security, even as the external world shifts.

The Vision of the Path Forward exercise invites practitioners to create an image of their intended path with the help of the Arcturian crystal. They hold the crystal at the third eye, and in this meditative state, they visualize a path stretching before them, one that feels aligned with their highest self. They imagine the crystal illuminating this path, casting light on each step ahead, however tentative or undefined it may be. This practice is about connecting with the intuition and inner wisdom that lie beneath the uncertainties, allowing the Arcturian crystal to act as a light in times of darkness, giving form to the vision of their future.

Sometimes, transitions require inner strength to release attachments. The Letting Go Ceremony uses the Arcturian crystal to facilitate this gentle release. Holding the crystal with both hands, practitioners visualize a part of themselves that they feel ready to let go—a thought pattern, a past attachment, or an emotional weight. They offer this part to the crystal, envisioning it gently dissolving within the crystal's energy. As they perform this ceremony, they repeat an affirmation like "I release what no longer serves my path forward." The crystal becomes a vessel for this letting go, transforming what is released into pure light, freeing the practitioner's energy for the new.

When emotions run high in times of change, the Inner Sanctuary Visualization provides a comforting refuge within. Practitioners hold the Arcturian crystal and envision a safe, serene sanctuary—this can be a space within the heart, or a landscape in nature. They see themselves entering this sanctuary with the crystal in hand, feeling its energy blend with the tranquility of the space. Here, they find calm and refuge, letting the crystal's presence ground them deeply. This sanctuary, formed by the connection with the Arcturian crystal, becomes a place they can return to whenever the need for stability arises.

For those seeking to connect with their intuition during transitions, the Guided Insight Practice allows the Arcturian crystal to become a guide. Sitting quietly with the crystal on their lap, they ask for insight regarding their journey forward, trusting that whatever impressions come to them—whether feelings, visions, or inner knowing—are part of the guidance they seek. They observe these impressions without judgment, feeling the crystal's support as it opens pathways to their own inner wisdom. This practice deepens their connection to their intuition, fostering trust in their ability to navigate through change.

In moments of vulnerability, practitioners may choose the Shield of Light Activation to feel protected and secure. Holding the Arcturian crystal to their heart, they visualize a soft but resilient light expanding from the crystal, enveloping them in a gentle shield. This shield acts as a buffer, protecting their energy from external influences and helping them focus on their inner journey without distraction. They can reaffirm this shield daily, knowing that the crystal's light fortifies their own as they move through periods of growth and transformation.

Sometimes, transitions can feel isolating, and the need for emotional support is heightened. The Heart Connection Meditation encourages practitioners to hold the crystal over the heart and feel a sense of connection to all those who are undergoing similar transformations. In this practice, they allow the crystal's energy to connect them to a collective field of strength and compassion, feeling the shared experience of growth that connects all beings. This meditation provides comfort, reminding them that they are not alone on their journey and that support exists within the vast interconnected web of life.

The Path of Renewal Affirmations allows practitioners to work with the crystal's energy to affirm their commitment to personal growth. Holding the Arcturian crystal, they speak affirmations aloud, such as "I embrace change with courage," "I am open to new beginnings," or "Each step forward brings me closer to my true self." These affirmations, spoken with intention, allow the crystal's energy to merge with their voice, amplifying their resolve and aligning their thoughts with a path of renewal. Each affirmation strengthens the practitioner's alignment with their evolving path, preparing them to face future challenges with resilience.

In these ways, the Arcturian crystals become more than just stones; they are guiding lights, stabilizing anchors, and sources of comfort. Each technique offers an approach to ease the journey through change, fostering resilience and inner clarity. The practitioner's connection with the crystal deepens with each use, forming a lasting partnership as they embrace the changes that lie ahead.

In the journey of transitions, the Arcturian crystal becomes a steady, supportive companion, helping practitioners navigate the evolving landscape of personal growth with wisdom and resilience. During times of profound change, practitioners may feel called to engage in structured practices that honor the past while empowering them to step forward with courage. This phase builds upon earlier techniques, offering practices designed to stabilize, renew, and empower the practitioner as they move through transformation with grace.

For many, moving forward first requires a conscious release of what no longer aligns. The *Ritual of Closure* provides a way for practitioners to honor the past without holding onto it. In a quiet space, they sit with their Arcturian crystal, reflecting on the aspects of life they feel ready to release—such as past relationships, outdated beliefs, or unfulfilled dreams. Holding the crystal in their hands, they connect with its grounding energy, visualizing these aspects dissolving into light. As they release each attachment, they acknowledge it with gratitude for its past role, then gently let it go, sensing the crystal's energy transmuting these attachments into wisdom and peace.

Once release has been honored, the Invocation of New Beginnings welcomes the energy of renewal into the practitioner's life. Holding the Arcturian crystal, they set intentions for what they wish to cultivate in the new phase. As they speak each intention aloud—whether it is courage, openness, or joy—they visualize the crystal absorbing their words, charging them with Arcturian energy. This practice anchors these intentions deeply, setting them into motion with the crystal as a witness and ally. Practitioners return to this invocation regularly to realign with their goals, letting the crystal's energy amplify their intentions as they take form.

When the path forward appears clouded by uncertainty, practitioners can rely on the Inner Compass Meditation to rediscover their inner direction. In a quiet state, they hold the Arcturian crystal at the center of their chest and close their eyes. They imagine it as a compass, aligned perfectly with their true purpose, and ask for guidance on the choices that lie ahead. As they breathe, they may notice subtle impressions, feelings, or insights—intuitive nudges pointing them in a certain direction. They allow these impressions to arise naturally, trusting that the crystal's energy will help bring their inner knowing to the surface. This technique helps them connect deeply with their intuition, revealing paths they may not have consciously considered.

Transformational Journaling is a practice that combines the power of self-reflection with the Arcturian crystal's ability to amplify insight. Practitioners hold the crystal beside them as they journal about the transition they're experiencing, asking questions like "What have I learned from this period of change?" or "What qualities do I need to cultivate for the journey ahead?" As they write, they visualize the crystal infusing their words with clarity and understanding, helping them access deeper layers of awareness. Over time, these entries form a record of their growth, capturing the wisdom that the transition brings, and allowing the crystal's energy to guide their reflections with a gentle, focused light.

For transitions marked by emotional intensity, the Gentle Release Breathwork technique provides a safe, healing space for processing emotions. Holding the Arcturian crystal in their lap, practitioners focus on slow, deliberate breaths. With each inhale, they draw in the crystal's calming energy; with each exhale, they release any feelings of tension, sadness, or fear. This rhythmic breathing allows the crystal's energy to merge with their own, creating a peaceful flow that softens emotional intensity. Over time, they may feel a sense of lightness, as if the crystal is gently lifting the weight of their emotions, allowing them to see the situation with newfound clarity.

The Alignment with Higher Purpose Visualization brings the practitioner's journey into perspective by connecting them with their greater purpose. They hold the Arcturian crystal at the third eye, closing their eyes to visualize a bright, golden path stretching before them—a path uniquely theirs, woven with the essence of their higher purpose. They imagine the crystal illuminating this path, revealing how the current transition fits within the broader journey of their life. This practice allows them to see the transition not as an isolated challenge but as a meaningful step in a larger tapestry. With each use, the practitioner gains perspective, feeling the crystal's reassurance that this period of change is essential for their growth.

In times of profound change, practitioners may feel drawn to the Crystalline Energy Grid technique, creating a personal grid of multiple Arcturian crystals around them. In this practice, they arrange crystals in a circle and sit within it, allowing themselves to be surrounded by the collective energy of the stones. As they sit, they visualize the grid as a cocoon of light, enveloping them with warmth, protection, and resilience. They may feel this grid absorbing and transforming any stress, confusion, or emotional upheaval, leaving them grounded and renewed. This technique is especially helpful during major life transitions, offering a stable energetic space in which they can process and integrate the changes.

Intention Setting with Elemental Energy is another practice that invites the elements—earth, water, fire, and air—to support the transition. Practitioners place their Arcturian crystal outside, connecting it with the natural elements: perhaps buried slightly in the earth, placed in a bowl of water, exposed briefly to a flame, or held up to the breeze. As they set an intention for each element (e.g., grounding with earth, cleansing with water), they allow the crystal to absorb these elemental energies, blending them into its own. When they retrieve the crystal, they hold it with a sense of completeness, knowing it now carries the transformative qualities of nature itself, ready to support them through every stage of their journey.

For those who seek resilience in the face of challenge, the Empowerment Mantra Meditation infuses the crystal's energy with affirmations. Practitioners hold the Arcturian crystal and repeat affirmations aloud, such as "I am resilient and adaptable," "I trust in my journey," or "This transition brings me closer to my true self." With each repetition, they visualize the crystal absorbing and magnifying the words, creating a powerful field of energy that surrounds them. This practice strengthens their resolve, allowing them to carry the affirmations within them, fortified by the crystal's resonance.

Cycle of Renewal Ritual honors the cyclical nature of life, allowing practitioners to recognize the natural flow of beginnings and endings. With their Arcturian crystal, they step into nature or sit by a window where they can feel connected to the seasons. Holding the crystal, they reflect on how each season brings change—spring's growth, summer's abundance, autumn's release, and winter's rest. They acknowledge their current place in this cycle, trusting that, like the seasons, their transition is part of an ongoing cycle of renewal. This ritual allows them to see change as part of a natural rhythm, one that leads to continual growth and evolution.

As practitioners engage with these advanced techniques, they find a deeper strength and resilience rising within them. Each practice brings new insights, gentle releases, and a growing confidence to embrace change as a path to transformation. The Arcturian crystal remains by their side, a steady source of light and energy, guiding them through the unknown with the wisdom that every ending is a doorway to something new, every transition a gift of evolution.

Chapter 24
Self-Confidence

There is a subtle power within the Arcturian crystals, a strength that resonates with the very core of self-assurance. For those embarking on a journey to cultivate self-confidence, these crystals act as allies, amplifying inner light and reinforcing a deep, unwavering trust in oneself. In every individual lies a potential to embody confidence that is rooted not in external validation but in an authentic, intrinsic knowing. The Arcturian crystals guide practitioners to unlock this reservoir of self-belief, revealing a profound courage that exists at the soul's center.

Self-confidence begins with an intimate connection to one's true self, an ability to stand firm in one's own value regardless of external circumstances. The Mirror of Self-Worth Meditation invites practitioners to hold their Arcturian crystal close to their heart, taking slow, deep breaths until a gentle calmness fills their mind. In this state, they visualize a mirror before them, one that reflects not the outer self but the essence of their spirit—strong, radiant, and resilient. As they gaze into this inner mirror, they affirm, "I am whole, and I am enough." They feel the crystal amplifying this energy, creating a sense of worthiness that radiates outward. Over time, this practice helps them embrace an unshakeable belief in their inherent value.

To further root this confidence, practitioners may turn to the Strength in Silence Practice. In a quiet, reflective space, they sit with the Arcturian crystal resting in their palm or at the base of their spine, feeling its energy flow through them. As they focus on the crystal's presence, they invite silence to fill their mind, releasing any thoughts or worries that might distract them from their inner strength. In this silence, they become acutely aware of the crystal's quiet power, a reminder that true strength does not need to announce itself. This practice helps them cultivate a steady, unspoken confidence, grounded in the simple knowledge of who they are.

For moments when doubt arises, the Empowerment Affirmation Technique helps reinforce confidence through spoken intention. Holding the crystal close, they choose affirmations that resonate deeply, such as "I trust in my abilities," "I am capable and resilient," or "I am confident in my path." Speaking each affirmation with conviction, they imagine the crystal absorbing and amplifying these words, sending waves of supportive energy through their being. The crystal becomes a vessel for these affirmations, storing them within its energy so that the practitioner can access this confidence whenever needed, simply by holding the crystal again.

At times, self-confidence is nurtured through a connection with the body, as physical awareness often serves as a foundation for emotional and mental strength. The Crystal Embodiment Practice invites practitioners to move mindfully with the crystal in hand, perhaps through gentle stretching or simple yoga poses. As they move, they feel the crystal's energy merging with their physical presence, encouraging a sense of harmony and balance. They let the crystal's energy remind them that confidence is not only a mental state but a felt presence in their body. This practice helps them embody self-assurance, cultivating a confidence that is grounded and physically integrated.

The Path of Inner Clarity Visualization is a technique for those seeking to deepen self-trust, which is a cornerstone of true confidence. Practitioners close their eyes with the crystal in their hands, visualizing a clear path stretching out before them. This path symbolizes the journey of their life, illuminated by the crystal's light, which reveals their own clarity and wisdom guiding each step. They envision themselves walking this path with certainty, trusting in their ability to navigate challenges and decisions along the way. This visualization strengthens their sense of inner clarity, reinforcing the belief that they possess all they need within themselves to move forward confidently.

For individuals who struggle with external criticism or judgment, the Energy Shield of Confidence offers a powerful layer of protection. Practitioners hold the crystal near their solar plexus, the energy center associated with personal power. They visualize a shield of light emanating from the crystal, surrounding them in a protective aura that reflects negativity and judgment back out, allowing only supportive energy to pass through. This shield acts as a reminder that their confidence need not be influenced by external opinions. Over time, this practice fosters resilience, enabling them to maintain self-assurance regardless of external challenges.

The Voice of Truth Practice helps practitioners cultivate the confidence to express themselves authentically. Holding the Arcturian crystal near their throat, they visualize it resonating with their voice, strengthening their ability to speak clearly and truthfully. They practice speaking aloud—whether affirmations, intentions, or even simple expressions of gratitude—feeling the crystal's energy supporting each word. This practice encourages them to express themselves without fear, knowing their voice is strong and worthy of being heard. Over time, this reinforces their ability to communicate with confidence and clarity in all areas of life.

For those who feel their confidence waver in the presence of others, the Self-Assurance Anchor is a grounding technique that reconnects them to their inner strength. In this practice, they carry the Arcturian crystal in a pocket or wear it as a pendant, and whenever they feel uncertain or overshadowed, they reach for it. Touching the crystal acts as an anchor, bringing them back to their center. They take a deep breath, allowing the crystal's energy to remind them of their own worth, fortifying them in the moment. This subtle, empowering gesture cultivates a quiet yet powerful confidence that they carry with them into any situation.

The Light of Self-Recognition Meditation is a practice designed to honor one's achievements and strengths, cultivating a sense of self-confidence through self-recognition. Practitioners sit with the crystal, reflecting on the qualities they appreciate in themselves, the moments they are proud of, and the growth they have achieved. Holding the crystal close, they imagine its energy expanding to reflect all these positive aspects back to them. This meditation fosters an inner recognition that is essential to lasting self-confidence, reinforcing the understanding that their value comes from within.

Lastly, the Inner Resilience Mantra is a way to anchor self-confidence through repeated practice. Practitioners choose a mantra that resonates, such as "I am confident, capable, and complete," and, while holding the crystal, repeat it silently or aloud. With each repetition, they visualize the crystal's energy blending with their own, strengthening their belief in themselves. This mantra becomes a touchstone, a source of empowerment that they can turn to whenever they need to reaffirm their self-assurance. The crystal's energy serves as a constant reminder that confidence is a steady, internal force, resilient against the tides of life.

As practitioners engage with these practices, the Arcturian crystal becomes more than a mere tool; it becomes a guide to discovering and deepening their own self-worth. Confidence, they come to realize, is not something that must be sought externally but is instead a profound, inner strength cultivated through self-awareness, trust, and resilience. With each practice, the crystal's energy supports them in recognizing the power within, encouraging them to step into the world with authenticity, courage, and the quiet assurance that they are, indeed, enough.

Deepening the journey to authentic self-confidence, practitioners find in the Arcturian crystal a steadfast source of reassurance—a quiet yet potent reminder of their inherent strength. While Part 1 introduced foundational practices, this phase guides practitioners into advanced methods that cultivate unwavering inner trust, fortifying confidence even in the face of challenges. Through these techniques, the crystal's energy acts as an anchor, rooting them in self-belief, resilience, and a deep conviction that their unique voice deserves to be heard.

One of the most profound practices is the *Crystal of Empowerment Ceremony*, a formal ritual designed to initiate a deep commitment to self-confidence. In a quiet, dimly lit room, the practitioner places their Arcturian crystal before them, lighting a candle as a symbol of their intention to illuminate self-worth. In silence, they reflect on qualities they wish to strengthen within themselves—whether it be courage, resilience, or self-acceptance. Holding the crystal in both hands, they speak aloud, affirming, "I am worthy. I am capable. I trust myself." They feel the crystal absorbing these words, charging with the energy of their intention. In this moment, the ceremony becomes a sacred vow, with the crystal as a committed ally in their journey toward self-confidence.

For situations where self-doubt is persistent, the Breaking the Chains Visualization offers a way to release limiting beliefs. Practitioners hold the Arcturian crystal at their heart, visualizing any doubts, fears, or judgments as chains binding them. With each exhale, they imagine the crystal's energy dissolving these chains, breaking them one by one. As the chains release, they feel a lightness, a liberation from the weight of self-judgment. This visualization is repeated whenever self-doubt arises, gradually helping them transcend the limitations that once hindered their confidence.

The Radiance Expansion Exercise is a unique technique that allows practitioners to radiate their confidence outward, creating an aura of self-assurance. Holding the crystal, they close their eyes and focus on their heart center, visualizing a warm, golden light there. With each breath, they see this light expanding, filling their entire body and surrounding them in a luminous aura. They imagine this light shining with confidence, compassion, and clarity, allowing it to touch everyone they encounter. Over time, this exercise not only strengthens their self-assurance but also makes them feel more comfortable sharing their authentic selves with others.

In moments of personal or professional challenge, the Shield of Self-Belief offers protection against the influence of external negativity. Practitioners hold the Arcturian crystal before them, visualizing a protective shield of light surrounding them, infused with the crystal's strength. This shield reflects any negative energy or doubt directed at them, allowing only constructive energy to pass through. This practice is especially useful in situations where they might feel vulnerable to criticism, ensuring that their confidence remains intact, shielded from external influences.

For those desiring to deepen self-compassion as a foundation of confidence, the Inner Light Connection Ritual helps to reinforce the relationship they have with themselves. In this ritual, practitioners sit with the crystal, placing it gently over their heart center, and breathe deeply. They reflect on their journey, acknowledging both their strengths and their vulnerabilities without judgment. As they breathe, they feel the crystal's energy blending with their own, recognizing that self-acceptance is the root of true confidence. Over time, this ritual helps practitioners see their full selves—both strengths and imperfections—as valuable parts of their journey.

The Empowered Voice Practice supports practitioners in confidently expressing their truth. In this practice, they hold the crystal at their throat, breathing deeply as they set the intention to speak openly and honestly. As they breathe, they feel the crystal amplifying their inner voice, creating a space where they feel safe to express themselves. Practitioners may use this technique before conversations or situations where they feel nervous about sharing their perspective. Through consistent practice, they find that their voice gains strength and clarity, allowing them to communicate authentically and assertively.

A practice of grounding and resilience, the Rooted Presence Meditation helps practitioners cultivate stability and confidence that feels immovable. Sitting with the crystal at their base chakra, they visualize roots extending from them into the earth, anchoring them deeply. They feel the crystal's energy merging with the strength of these roots, providing a grounded foundation for their confidence. With each breath, they feel more centered, rooted, and unshakable. This practice is especially helpful in moments of uncertainty or instability, reinforcing the practitioner's inner strength as they face life's challenges.

In times of self-doubt, the Crystal Companion Reflection serves as a gentle yet powerful reminder of self-worth. Practitioners hold the crystal and gaze into it, allowing themselves to see their reflection within. They may speak softly to themselves, acknowledging their strengths and qualities they value. This simple yet meaningful practice builds a relationship of trust and appreciation with oneself, using the crystal as a mirror to remind them of their beauty and worth, creating a bond that grows stronger with each use.

For long-term confidence building, the Layered Intention Technique helps practitioners create a cumulative effect, layering their intentions for confidence over time. Each week, they hold the crystal and set a single, focused intention, such as "I trust in my decisions" or "I stand in my truth." As the weeks pass, they add new intentions, each one building upon the last. The crystal becomes a repository of these layered affirmations, serving as a concentrated source of self-confidence that they can draw upon whenever needed.

The Empowerment Through Action practice transforms intentions into reality by encouraging practitioners to take steps, however small, toward their goals. Holding the crystal, they set an intention to act with confidence, identifying a specific action they can take. This might be speaking up in a meeting, reaching out to someone new, or expressing an opinion they've held back. They carry the crystal with them as they take this action, feeling its energy as a source of courage. This practice reminds them that confidence grows not only through intention but through consistent, empowered action.

The Cycle of Reflection and Growth encourages practitioners to periodically review their journey, acknowledging the growth they have achieved and reinforcing their ongoing commitment to self-confidence. Every month, they hold the Arcturian crystal and reflect on moments where they exhibited confidence, large or small. They acknowledge these moments, feeling gratitude for their progress, and set intentions for areas they still wish to strengthen. This practice creates a continuous cycle of reflection and growth, allowing their confidence to evolve naturally over time, with the crystal as a steady, guiding presence.

In these advanced practices, practitioners find that the Arcturian crystal becomes an embodiment of their journey toward self-confidence. Each technique builds upon the next, forming a foundation that is both expansive and resilient, fortified through self-acceptance, self-expression, and a deep-rooted belief in their intrinsic worth. As they move forward, practitioners carry with them a quiet yet profound assurance that, with the crystal by their side, they are ready to stand confidently in the world, guided by the light of their own inner strength.

Chapter 25
Consciousness Expansion

In the quiet reach of night, as stars scatter across the boundless sky, the Arcturian crystals pulse with an invitation to expand consciousness, to venture beyond the boundaries of ordinary perception. Their energy acts as a bridge between realms, a channel through which seekers may glimpse dimensions beyond the mundane, meeting parts of themselves they might have long forgotten. Within the Arcturian frequency lies an invitation to embark on a journey into profound self-awareness, to the heart of universal wisdom, and to a vision of life elevated beyond habitual perceptions.

It begins with the Gateway of Stillness, a ritual designed to dissolve the illusions that bind the mind. As practitioners sit quietly with their crystal, they focus on their breath, allowing thoughts to pass like shadows across a vast landscape. The crystal, held gently in hand or placed at the heart, pulses with a calming, clarifying energy. Its essence leads the practitioner into stillness, a silence deep enough to hear whispers of the cosmos. The mind begins to empty, making space for new insights to arise, opening consciousness to truths that cannot be spoken yet are felt profoundly. This stillness becomes a portal, allowing glimpses into a self that exists beyond time and space.

As they proceed, they may find themselves drawn to the Sky Mirror Visualization. With this technique, the Arcturian crystal becomes a tool of reflection—an instrument that mirrors the vastness of the universe within. Practitioners close their eyes, holding the crystal in one hand, and visualize a vast sky filled with stars, each point of light representing a facet of their consciousness. As they hold this image, the stars begin to move, shifting into patterns and forming constellations unique to their inner landscape. Each constellation holds a memory, a wisdom, a dream. As they focus on these shapes, they find answers to questions buried within, pieces of self emerging from distant points of awareness.

For those seeking an even deeper immersion, the Eclipse of the Self practice offers a way to step outside of identity entirely, to experience the vastness of consciousness unfiltered by personal boundaries. Holding the crystal to the brow, the practitioner visualizes themselves in the center of a darkened sky, where the light of a powerful sun is eclipsed behind a passing moon. In this silence, they feel the presence of the infinite, realizing the unity that connects all beings. In this moment, individuality fades, replaced by a profound sense of interconnectedness, as if they are both the sun and the moon, the seeker and the knowledge, all at once.

In times of heightened insight, the Crystal Lens Exercise allows practitioners to sharpen their awareness and sense clarity in the wisdom they encounter. This practice involves placing the crystal over the third eye and envisioning it as a lens through which the universe is seen in its true form. As they focus, they find that colors become richer, sounds softer, and thoughts more precise. The crystal's energy filters distractions, enabling a crystalline clarity of thought and feeling. This exercise becomes a guide, allowing practitioners to sift through the endless stream of experiences, perceiving only those that resonate with their higher self.

The Labyrinth of Light Journey beckons those who are ready to explore the inner landscape more actively. Practitioners envision themselves entering a labyrinth made entirely of light, each turn revealing new facets of their consciousness. Holding the crystal close, they walk through corridors of memory, meeting parts of themselves hidden by time, releasing burdens they may not have realized they were carrying. This journey often culminates in a central chamber bathed in radiant light, where the essence of their truest self awaits. This practice is one of inner reconciliation, bringing together the fragments of the self into a harmonious whole.

The Celestial Harmonization Technique aids practitioners in connecting their energy with the rhythm of the cosmos, aligning their consciousness with celestial cycles. On a star-filled night, they sit beneath the sky, holding their crystal and focusing on a specific star or constellation. They allow its light to merge with the crystal, which they then hold close, feeling the alignment between their pulse and the far-off celestial body. This exercise fosters an understanding that they are part of a greater cosmic rhythm, that their consciousness expands outward, touching realms as vast as the heavens above.

For those inclined toward dreamwork, the Nocturnal Exploration practice is a way to channel the Arcturian crystal's energy into the subconscious. Before sleep, practitioners hold the crystal, setting an intention for clarity in their dreams. As they drift into sleep, they feel the crystal guiding their consciousness into a state of lucid receptivity. Dreams may become more vivid, revealing insights veiled by waking life, offering symbols and messages that lead to self-discovery. This practice often brings the practitioner a sense of continuity, as if the dream world is not separate but an extension of their conscious journey.

The Temple of Reflection Ritual is designed for those moments when practitioners seek a quiet sanctuary within themselves, a space where they can return to their highest truth. Sitting with the crystal in a dimly lit room, they create an inner temple—a space of peace and wisdom. Within this temple, they place the crystal on an imagined altar, lighting a candle within their mind's eye. Here, they sit, breathe, and feel the deep resonance of their inner sanctuary. Each visit to this inner temple strengthens their awareness, expanding their consciousness with each session, making it easier to return to this state of calm clarity in daily life.

With time and practice, each of these techniques builds upon the other, creating a pathway to expanded awareness that leads practitioners into the realms of intuition, insight, and boundless wisdom. The Arcturian crystal, more than just a guide, becomes a symbol of the limitless potential within. As practitioners deepen their connection to this energy, they find their consciousness flowering, each petal revealing new dimensions, guiding them to truths that can only be found when one surrenders to the mystery of the universe within.

With every journey into consciousness comes a recognition of its boundless nature. Just as the stars remain undiscovered in their entirety, the layers of human awareness, aided by the resonance of Arcturian crystals, hold infinite potential for exploration. To those prepared to immerse themselves, each Arcturian crystal is a beacon, illuminating inner spaces and creating channels that reveal new ways of perceiving and experiencing existence.

A vital technique in this journey is the Veil of Perception Ritual. This practice begins with a gentle cleanse of the crystal to prepare it for deep meditative work. Once seated comfortably, the practitioner places the crystal against the third eye and visualizes a delicate veil that separates the visible from the hidden. By mentally drawing aside this veil, they allow visions, symbols, and impressions to come forward. These may be abstract—a color, a sound, or a sudden clarity about an unresolved matter. Through this veil, practitioners find that the ordinary world of senses begins to merge with an intuitive, symbol-laden language unique to the Arcturian realm.

Another method of consciousness expansion emerges through the Radiance of Spheres exercise. Here, practitioners envision the Arcturian crystal as the center of expanding circles of energy, each circle representing a sphere of awareness. Starting with the immediate, personal sphere, they visualize layers expanding outward—family, community, humanity, and finally, the cosmos. As each layer expands, practitioners connect with the consciousness that each sphere represents, feeling the interwoven nature of all existence. In this practice, the crystal aids in dissolving individual boundaries, allowing practitioners to feel part of the collective soul.

For deeper access to intuitive insights, the Crystal Gateway to Timelessness beckons. Holding the Arcturian crystal, practitioners set the intention to connect with a timeless dimension. This exercise may reveal past events, memories, or insights that feel strangely familiar yet carry a weight of timeless wisdom. The crystal acts as an anchor, guiding practitioners through memories or ancient symbols that arise unbidden, each offering a fragment of understanding about the continuous thread of consciousness through time.

The Unified Breath of Stars involves breathing in rhythm with the imagined pulse of a distant star or planet, the crystal pressed close to the heart or the crown. Practitioners visualize the chosen celestial body's light flowing into the crystal and their own breath, merging as one. Each inhale draws this celestial light into their being, and each exhale sends the energy back outward, a perpetual exchange between self and the universe. This practice creates a sense of unity with celestial bodies, fostering a tangible connection to the vastness of existence that lies beyond the personal self.

The Transcendent Mirror Technique introduces another facet of consciousness expansion. Practitioners place the crystal in front of them, at eye level, as if it were a mirror reflecting their true self. With deep focus, they imagine seeing not the physical self, but the essence of who they are at a spiritual level. As they observe this reflection, they may notice changes in color, shape, or even the crystal's energy frequency—a visual metaphor for the soul's essence. This reflection grows clearer with each session, gradually transforming the way they perceive their inner self and unlocking hidden aspects of consciousness.

In moments of profound exploration, practitioners may be drawn to the Chamber of Etheric Light meditation. In this practice, they envision themselves entering a chamber of translucent light, suspended in ether. The crystal amplifies the chamber's vibrational resonance, enveloping the practitioner in an aura of radiant, shifting colors. This etheric light penetrates the energetic body, each color representing a different aspect of cosmic knowledge or wisdom. This chamber serves as a place of reflection and rejuvenation, allowing practitioners to release limitations, shifting their consciousness into an entirely new frequency.

Another powerful method, the Tapestry of Dreams and Visions, encourages practitioners to work with the crystal during sleep. Before bed, they hold the crystal, setting a clear intention to receive guidance or visions. Throughout the night, the Arcturian energy flows through the dream state, and as practitioners wake, they record the dreams immediately, noticing patterns, symbols, or insights that arise. Over time, these dream journals become a tapestry of inner knowledge, each thread revealing a piece of the broader consciousness woven through their lives.

The Harmonic Sound of Silence practice requires deep concentration, merging the crystal's frequency with the practitioner's inner resonance. Sitting in silence, they hold the crystal to the heart and close their eyes, listening not to external sounds but to the pulse within. They may begin to feel subtle vibrations, harmonies that emerge from the silence, as if the crystal's energy has unlocked a hidden frequency. This soundless resonance becomes a teacher, guiding practitioners into realms beyond words or symbols, where consciousness expands without boundaries.

For the mystic in search of clarity on their path, the Celestial Compass exercise reveals a guiding direction. Practitioners place the crystal at the center of a small, circular space and stand on its edge, walking slowly around, envisioning each step as a journey through life stages or challenges. At moments of pause, they look toward the crystal, seeking answers within its depths. This compass provides orientation, a way to return to one's center, trusting that the crystal holds an answer to each question posed.

As practitioners continue this path, they find that these exercises are more than a journey; they are a reawakening to the multidimensional self, the limitless awareness that the Arcturian crystal reveals. With each meditation, breath, and vision, their consciousness unfolds, like petals of an ancient flower long dormant, greeting the light. The crystal, with its Arcturian frequency, becomes both map and guide, leading them ever deeper into the sanctuary of cosmic unity and self-realization.

Chapter 26
Inner Balance

In the delicate tapestry of existence, inner balance serves as the quiet anchor within the storm, a place of stability that allows for clarity and peace even in turbulent moments. Arcturian crystals, with their deeply harmonizing energy, guide practitioners to this center—a place where emotions settle and the mind stills, fostering an unwavering calm. The journey toward inner balance is not one of resistance but of gentle acceptance, a practice of aligning with the quiet currents beneath the surface.

The Harmonic Heart Alignment is one such practice that opens the doorway to balance. Sitting with the crystal against the heart, practitioners close their eyes and envision the crystal's gentle frequency pulsing in rhythm with their heartbeat. With each pulse, the Arcturian energy flows through the heart, clearing emotional blockages and creating a field of tranquility that expands outward. This rhythm becomes an internal melody, aligning the heart and emotions, encouraging practitioners to experience feelings without being overwhelmed. The crystal amplifies this alignment, allowing the heart to regain its natural harmony.

The Waves of Breath technique is another powerful exercise, one that fosters balance through conscious breathing. Holding the crystal, practitioners take deep breaths, imagining the energy of the crystal merging with each inhale, creating a rhythm that mirrors gentle ocean waves. With each exhale, they release any stored tension or worry. This flow of breath encourages a natural ebb and flow of energy, guiding them to experience calmness that originates from within. In moments of chaos, they return to this wave-like breath, feeling the soothing presence of the crystal's energy, their inner equilibrium restored.

A deeply grounding practice, Rooting with the Earth, calls practitioners to place the crystal near the base of the spine or between their palms, sitting cross-legged on the ground. They envision roots growing from the crystal into the earth, drawing up stability and resilience. As these roots deepen, practitioners visualize the earth's energy mingling with the Arcturian crystal's frequency, forming an unbreakable connection to the core of the earth. This practice grounds the spirit, balancing the physical and energetic bodies, reminding them of the interconnectedness of all things. It is from this grounding that they can find stability within their being, regardless of external shifts.

The Mirror of Self-Acceptance exercise is a journey into the often-unseen aspects of oneself. Practitioners sit with the crystal and focus on their reflection within its facets, seeking not only to see their physical self but to gaze deeper. This reflection becomes a meditation on self-acceptance, a recognition of both strengths and vulnerabilities. With each breath, they allow the crystal's energy to wash over any judgments or insecurities, releasing them into the light. In this mirror, practitioners come to see their true selves, imperfections and all, held within the gentle energy of the Arcturian crystal, finding balance in self-compassion.

For those moments when the mind races, or when the heart feels heavy, The Balanced Bridge technique serves as a powerful intermediary. Practitioners hold the crystal with both hands, bringing it to the center of their chest, focusing on the space between heart and mind. They breathe deeply, feeling the crystal as a bridge that connects these two centers, encouraging thoughts and emotions to meet in harmony. This technique balances mental clarity with emotional insight, guiding practitioners toward decisions and thoughts that reflect inner peace.

The Centering Spiral is a visualization exercise that draws the mind into a single point of focus, creating an immediate sense of calm. Sitting with the crystal, practitioners envision a spiral beginning at the crystal's center and moving outward. With each turn of the spiral, they feel themselves drawn deeper into stillness, as thoughts and distractions drift away. This spiral of energy, infused with the crystal's frequency, brings the practitioner's awareness to their inner center, a place where silence and stability dwell. In this quiet center, they feel balanced, shielded from the disturbances of the outside world.

In moments of high stress or anxiety, the Orb of Tranquility technique offers a safe harbor. Practitioners hold the crystal close to their heart and visualize a soft orb of light surrounding their body, infused with the crystal's energy. This orb grows with each breath, creating a cocoon of serenity. Within this orb, practitioners find that worries and fears dissipate, replaced by a sense of calm that permeates their being. This tranquility orb can be called upon at any moment, surrounding the practitioner in a field of peace, balancing both body and spirit.

The Essence of Still Waters exercise invites practitioners to engage with the crystal while focusing on the metaphor of still water. Holding the crystal, they envision their thoughts and emotions as ripples on the surface of a lake. As they breathe, they imagine the ripples slowly settling, until the water is perfectly calm and reflective. The crystal amplifies this visualization, guiding practitioners to a state of inner stillness where they can observe their thoughts without being pulled into them. It is here that true balance is found—a state of calm observation and presence.

The Chimes of Harmony is a practice that incorporates sound and vibration. Practitioners gently tap the crystal, listening to the subtle chime it produces or imagining its vibrational tone. They allow this sound to resonate within them, feeling the crystal's frequency harmonize with their own. Each tap and each chime clears lingering energies, creating a field of balance and harmony that lingers long after the sound has faded. This practice attunes them to the rhythm of the crystal, connecting them to a deeper resonance within themselves.

Through these practices, practitioners come to understand that balance is not a state to be achieved once but a continual process of realignment, much like the movement of celestial bodies. In their connection with Arcturian crystals, they find not just tools, but guides that support this journey toward harmony and stillness. Each moment spent with these crystals becomes an affirmation of the natural rhythm within, a return to the quiet equilibrium that lies beneath the surface of life.

As the practitioner deepens their journey toward inner balance, the Arcturian crystal becomes a steadfast companion, guiding them through layers of self-awareness and grounding. This part of the journey goes beyond achieving balance momentarily; it seeks to infuse every aspect of life with a sense of equilibrium, a subtle, resilient harmony that endures through change and challenge.

The Unified Flow is a practice that unites the physical and energetic bodies, a dance between the breath, movement, and the crystal's energy. Practitioners hold the crystal, and with each inhalation, they lift it toward the sky, feeling a connection to the energy above. With each exhalation, they bring it back down toward the earth, feeling its grounding strength. This rhythmic motion aligns their inner world with the vastness of the universe, creating a harmony between the energy centers in the body. In this flow, they find their inner balance attuned not only to themselves but to the cosmic energies surrounding them.

An exercise called Eternal Horizon teaches practitioners to see beyond temporary circumstances, training the mind to find stability in the ever-changing waves of life. Holding the crystal, they sit quietly and visualize a vast, open horizon stretching infinitely. With each breath, they allow their worries to drift toward this horizon, watching as they dissipate into the distance. In moments of imbalance or uncertainty, this exercise offers a reminder that all things pass, but inner peace remains, like the horizon itself. This practice of letting go allows the crystal to amplify a state of unwavering tranquility, a balanced point amidst life's transitory nature.

The Elemental Resonance practice guides practitioners through a connection to the elements—earth, water, fire, and air—drawing on each to fortify their sense of balance. They sit in a circle with four crystals, each representing an element, surrounding them. With each breath, they envision one element's energy, feeling its qualities entering and balancing their energy field. Earth offers grounding, water brings fluidity, fire infuses warmth, and air brings clarity. With the Arcturian crystals as conduits, practitioners cultivate balance not only within themselves but with the natural world, attuning to its rhythm, drawing strength from the primal forces that sustain all life.

In the quietude of the Sacred Sphere, practitioners can find shelter from life's intensity. Sitting with the crystal, they close their eyes and envision a soft sphere of Arcturian light forming around them. This sphere encompasses them completely, creating an inner sanctuary where no external energies can disturb their peace. Inside this sphere, practitioners can process emotions, thoughts, and feelings without external interference. The Sacred Sphere becomes a space of balance—a personal realm where clarity and calm are ever-present, and where the crystal's energy flows uninterrupted, washing away discord.

For times when balance feels elusive, the Heart Compass practice returns practitioners to their center through guided intuition. Holding the crystal to their heart, they focus on a question or decision, allowing the crystal's frequency to connect them with their deeper wisdom. The crystal amplifies inner clarity, helping them to feel the subtle pull of their heart's direction. Rather than relying solely on logic, this practice fosters balance between mind and heart, creating a centered and wise perspective that guides them toward harmonious choices.

The Harmony Web is a powerful group practice that deepens the experience of interconnected balance. Practitioners sit in a circle, each holding an Arcturian crystal, and connect through a shared visualization of energy lines linking each crystal, forming a web of harmony. As they breathe together, they visualize their energies joining through this web, reinforcing each other's sense of peace and balance. This shared energy becomes a powerful force, allowing each practitioner to find equilibrium not only in themselves but in connection with others, recognizing that balance is strengthened through unity.

In the Serenity Pulse practice, practitioners place the crystal near their navel, the body's energetic center, while focusing on the rhythm of their heartbeat. Each heartbeat is visualized as a ripple of energy that the crystal amplifies and spreads throughout the body. This pulse becomes a steady anchor, harmonizing all energy centers with the natural rhythm of the body, allowing practitioners to carry a deep inner stillness with them wherever they go. In times of distress, the Serenity Pulse serves as a calming practice, a reminder of the constant, balanced rhythm of life itself.

The Mirror of Duality practice guides practitioners to embrace all aspects of themselves, balancing light and shadow. They sit before a mirror with the crystal in hand, gazing at their reflection and acknowledging both strengths and fears. They allow the crystal's energy to soften any judgments, embracing themselves wholly. This acceptance brings them into balance with their true nature, allowing them to see all aspects as necessary parts of their journey. Through the crystal, they find that peace arises not from denying the darker aspects of self but by harmonizing with them.

Celestial Alignment draws on the energy of the stars, using the crystal as a tool to connect to the broader cosmic cycles. Practitioners hold the crystal under the night sky, allowing its energy to absorb and resonate with starlight. They meditate on their connection to the universe, feeling themselves as part of the vast cosmic balance. In this state, they find that inner balance extends beyond themselves, a thread woven into the grand design of the cosmos. This practice instills a deep awareness of universal harmony, grounding them in a balanced state that aligns with the rhythm of the stars.

In quiet reflection, practitioners are invited to consider the Cycle of Renewal, aligning their inner energy with the natural cycles of life—birth, growth, release, and renewal. They sit with the crystal and visualize the current phase of their life, understanding it as a season within the greater cycle. Holding the crystal, they let go of energies they no longer need, allowing new energies to fill that space. The Arcturian crystal amplifies this renewal, connecting them with the ebb and flow of existence, helping them find balance in each phase of their journey.

The final technique, Inner Light Reverberation, involves a meditation where practitioners hold the crystal near their heart and visualize their inner light expanding outward. As this light meets the crystal, it is reflected back, intensifying and harmonizing with the practitioner's energy. In this exchange, they feel a growing sense of self-compassion and stability. This light becomes a constant, centered presence within, allowing them to maintain balance amid life's fluctuations.

Through these practices, practitioners deepen their ability to find inner balance not as a static state but as a continuous, dynamic process. The Arcturian crystals serve as both grounding anchors and guiding lights, leading practitioners to their center and teaching that balance, once found within, extends outward, creating harmony in every sphere of life. In this way, the journey toward balance becomes a path of quiet power, resilience, and boundless peace.

Chapter 27
Deep Meditation

Within the silence of deep meditation, the Arcturian crystal serves as a bridge between the physical and spiritual realms, guiding practitioners into profound states of inner peace and awareness. The journey begins with simple, intentional steps, deepening as practitioners surrender to the quietude, immersing themselves in the crystal's energy, allowing its frequency to resonate with the depths of their consciousness.

The Sacred Descent practice encourages a soft, gradual transition from wakefulness into a meditative state, holding the crystal as they sit comfortably, eyes gently closed. With each breath, they imagine sinking further into themselves, as if moving layer by layer deeper within. The crystal acts as an anchor, grounding the practitioner while helping them sink into inner stillness. The rhythm of each breath is the rhythm of descent, a soft falling into the quiet, where thoughts dissipate, leaving only the pulse of peace.

In Celestial Reflection, the crystal becomes a conduit for cosmic connection, amplifying the practitioner's awareness of the vastness of existence. They hold the crystal at their heart and visualize their inner light stretching outward to meet the stars. This practice evokes a sense of boundlessness, where individual awareness merges with the universe's expanse. In this space, meditation transforms into communion, a silent conversation between the soul and the cosmos, where personal insights arrive as whispers from the stars themselves, resonating with an understanding beyond words.

Another step deeper brings the Well of Stillness meditation, where practitioners focus on the crystal's frequency to reach a state of profound internal quiet. Placing the crystal near the center of their forehead, they imagine it radiating waves of stillness, calming all thoughts and emotions. This quiet intensifies, allowing them to drift inward to a place of pure silence, like reaching the bottom of a deep well. Here, there is nothing but serenity—a state in which even the subtle currents of thought disappear, leaving only the crystal's serene energy as a gentle presence.

The Chamber of Mirrors practice offers a unique form of self-exploration, guiding practitioners through a series of internal reflections. Holding the crystal, they mentally create a quiet chamber within themselves, one lined with mirrors reflecting every layer of their being. As they gaze into each reflection, the crystal helps them see clearly, with compassion, the aspects of themselves that lie hidden. This journey allows them to explore parts of the psyche, seeing each one with acceptance, learning to integrate every facet of their identity with harmony.

In Breath of the Stars, practitioners synchronize their breathing with the crystal's energy, breathing in a gentle light that fills the body, and exhaling all tensions and barriers. This practice cultivates a peaceful rhythm, where each breath feels like the quiet pulse of a distant star. The light, guided by the crystal's energy, fills each corner of the body, aligning every cell with a calming, cosmic vibration. This meditation allows practitioners to feel both profoundly grounded and infinitely expansive, embodying the vast peace of the universe within.

For Inner Oasis, practitioners sit with the crystal in both hands, holding it close to their heart. They visualize it as a seed from which an inner garden of tranquility blooms. In this sanctuary, surrounded by imagined greenery and gentle water, they feel shielded from the outside world, protected within the crystal's calming energy. This mental garden offers a safe space where they can let go of any burdens, a serene oasis that replenishes the spirit and restores peace, leaving them with a sense of inner nourishment and stillness.

A meditative practice known as the Golden Thread guides practitioners to follow an energetic line back through their memories and experiences. Holding the crystal, they visualize a golden thread stretching from their heart through the journey of their life. As they trace this thread, guided by the crystal's light, they pass each moment with gratitude, releasing any lingering attachments. The meditation becomes a way to travel backward while remaining centered in the present, finding closure and understanding in past experiences, reaching a point where they can hold these moments in peace, no longer bound by them.

The Veil of Light meditation encourages a state of complete energetic alignment. Practitioners close their eyes and visualize a veil of soft light flowing from the crystal, enveloping them gently. As the veil surrounds their entire being, they feel it harmonizing every part of their energy field, balancing every layer. This light veil acts as a filter, absorbing any residual energies that do not belong and leaving them with only their pure, unaltered essence. It is a practice of renewal, a return to their core, where their spirit stands clear and luminous.

Journey to the Source invites practitioners to use the crystal as a guide to explore the depths of their consciousness. Sitting in a comfortable position with the crystal at their brow, they envision themselves traveling within, moving deeper until they reach a source—a wellspring of pure, vibrant energy at the core of their being. This source holds the essence of who they are, untouched by time or experience. In this meditative state, they experience a reunion with their truest self, feeling a profound sense of belonging and completeness, as if they are finally home within themselves.

In Waves of Tranquility, practitioners visualize their breath as gentle waves flowing from the crystal, spreading through their entire body. As each wave travels, it releases any tension, anxiety, or distraction, leaving them with an undeniable sense of calm. This rhythm lulls them deeper, wave by wave, into a meditative state where they feel the steady presence of peace in every part of their being. Each wave of tranquility is a step into deeper awareness, carrying them effortlessly into the heart of stillness.

The Cradle of Timelessness meditation uses the crystal as a portal to step outside of ordinary time. With the crystal resting in their hands, they focus on its energy as a gateway to timelessness. Here, they become simply present, untouched by the past or future. In this state, they experience the clarity and peace that arise when time falls away—a profound, eternal moment where they feel both infinite and profoundly connected to the now.

For the Deep Resonance practice, practitioners sit in silence, focusing on the subtle hum of energy emanating from the crystal. They allow themselves to match this frequency, aligning every part of their being with this gentle, peaceful resonance. As they tune in, they experience a vibrational harmony that brings both mind and body into unity, a tranquil state of coherence where they feel the crystal's energy merging with their own.

Lastly, Threshold of the Spirit invites practitioners to the edge of their conscious awareness, sitting in the presence of the crystal while embracing the unknown. In this practice, they approach meditation as a journey to explore what lies beyond ordinary perception. The crystal acts as a guide to this threshold, a companion as they step beyond their usual boundaries into the mysteries of existence, finding not answers, but the comfort of feeling at peace with the unknown.

As practitioners move through these practices, the Arcturian crystal becomes a steadying force in the vastness of meditation, holding them gently as they dive into the depths of themselves. In these moments, they discover that deep meditation is more than a retreat from the world; it is a journey into the heart of the self, where peace waits eternally, ready to embrace them with the quiet wisdom of the universe.

Deep within the silent realms, the practitioner finds the crystal as both a bridge and a catalyst, guiding them toward increasingly subtle states of awareness. Here, meditation transforms into a journey of profound depth, where each practice becomes a doorway to layers of understanding hidden beyond ordinary sight. The crystal's energy is a companion in this descent, and as it gently aligns with the practitioner's inner rhythm, it awakens a presence that transcends time and space.

In Sanctuary of Stillness, the crystal acts as a beacon guiding practitioners through a visualization of entering a quiet, sacred sanctuary within themselves. The world beyond falls away, replaced by the tranquil sound of silence. As they visualize a calm space filled with light, they find themselves in a realm where thought and distraction cannot follow. The sanctuary becomes a wellspring of clarity, where stillness deepens with each breath. The presence of the crystal intensifies this experience, creating a cocoon of peace that shields and nurtures the practitioner in pure serenity.

Another step forward brings the Echo of the Cosmos practice, an exercise in cosmic reflection. Sitting with the crystal at their heart, practitioners visualize themselves as part of the vast expanse, feeling the pulse of the universe in perfect synchrony with their own heartbeat. Each beat echoes across the cosmos, merging personal awareness with the infinite. The crystal amplifies this sensation, dissolving the boundary between self and the universe, leaving only a vast and interconnected awareness, like stardust spread across the fabric of existence.

The Pathway of Light practice encourages practitioners to follow a stream of inner light emanating from the crystal, guiding them along an ethereal pathway. This light moves gently, drawing them deeper, with each step releasing thoughts, emotions, and attachments. As they follow, they arrive at a place beyond mental constructs—a place of profound purity and peace. Here, there is no need for language or thought, only the quiet knowledge that they have reached a space of true inner freedom.

In the Mirror of Reflection, practitioners hold the crystal and envision it as a mirror reflecting the essence of their soul. Each image that appears in the crystal's mirror is a glimpse into an aspect of themselves, sometimes hidden or unacknowledged. With patience, they examine each reflection, learning to see without judgment, embracing the entirety of their being. This practice fosters self-acceptance, helping them to reconcile with all aspects of their identity, standing in unity with their own spirit.

The Celestial Heartbeat practice uses the crystal to attune the practitioner's energy to the natural rhythms of the universe. Holding the crystal near the heart, they visualize each beat as an alignment with the pulse of cosmic energy flowing through all creation. This rhythm connects them to the stars, planets, and the unseen forces binding the universe. In this quiet, rhythmic union, they find a sense of belonging to the vast tapestry of life, where they are neither separate nor isolated, but an integral part of a beautiful, harmonious whole.

In Journey to the Inner Sea, practitioners visualize an ocean within, a sea of their own consciousness. As they enter this inner sea, they float upon its gentle waves, feeling the crystal as a weight that anchors them safely within this tranquil space. Each wave calms and clears, leaving them free of thought, bathed in the deep and endless ocean of peace. The crystal's frequency melds with the currents, guiding them through this inner world, allowing them to sink gently into a place where they are both the observer and the observed.

With the Starry Veil, practitioners visualize themselves draped in a veil of starlight emanating from the crystal, each star representing a moment, a memory, or a piece of wisdom. They feel the gentle weight of this veil, connecting them to the vast reservoir of knowledge within themselves. As they rest in this cosmic cloak, they sense insights arising, not as mental revelations, but as a quiet understanding that surfaces naturally, merging with their consciousness, leaving them feeling wise, clear, and whole.

The Path of the Seeker meditation is a journey through the inner mysteries, where the crystal serves as a lantern in the dark. Holding the crystal, practitioners enter a mental pathway, following its light as it illuminates forgotten parts of themselves.

Along this path, they encounter moments from the past, potential futures, and hidden dreams. This path encourages exploration without fear, for the light of the crystal ensures that they are always safe, helping them return with new insights into their journey of self-discovery.

In The River of Time, the crystal becomes a tool for moving through the flow of memories and experiences. Practitioners visualize themselves standing by a river, where each ripple is a moment from their life. As they gaze into the water, they see scenes from the past and potential glimpses of the future. The crystal's energy allows them to move freely along this river, pausing to reflect on any moment. In this timeless space, they see how all experiences connect, merging into a coherent whole, offering clarity and a deep sense of continuity.

The Gates of Eternity practice allows practitioners to experience a sense of boundless time. Holding the crystal, they enter a state where moments dissolve, and they become aware of an eternal presence within. This presence, untouched by the past or future, is an experience of pure consciousness, beyond the ordinary limits of time. In this state, they feel both profoundly connected to all that has been and free of any constraints, touching upon the timeless essence of the self, a connection with the eternal core of existence.

For The Well of Memory, practitioners envision the crystal as a well filled with reflections from their past. As they peer into this well, they see moments both joyful and challenging. The crystal's energy helps them to embrace each image, recognizing it as part of their journey, drawing lessons and insights from each one. This gentle reflection allows them to honor all that has been, to release any lingering emotions, and to carry forward only the wisdom these moments have imparted.

The Light of Unity meditation guides practitioners to experience themselves as a single note in a vast cosmic symphony. Holding the crystal, they imagine its energy as a unifying force, blending their essence with the energy of the universe. They are no longer isolated but a part of a larger harmony, feeling every thought, action, and breath as part of a universal rhythm. This practice dissolves feelings of separation, awakening a profound sense of unity and oneness with all existence.

In Threshold of the Soul, the crystal helps practitioners approach a place within themselves where the known meets the unknown. Sitting quietly with the crystal, they feel as if they are standing on the edge of a vast, mysterious realm. They are not here to seek answers, but simply to be present at this threshold, embracing the mystery. The crystal's energy supports them in this space, allowing them to feel at peace with the unknown, finding beauty in the openness and silence.

Lastly, Resonance of Tranquility brings practitioners into a state of profound internal harmony. They imagine the crystal's energy as waves that flow through them, gently tuning every part of their being to the frequency of peace. As they breathe in this tranquility, they feel each cell, each thought, each feeling align with this calm resonance. The meditation becomes an immersion into pure peace, a deep state of coherence where mind, body, and spirit merge seamlessly into the quiet hum of existence.

In these meditative practices, the crystal serves as a sacred companion, guiding practitioners not only into themselves but beyond the confines of self. With each journey, they venture into a state where they discover that the limits they perceive in daily life are but thin veils, gently lifted through meditation. Here, the crystal is more than a tool; it becomes a bridge to realms within and beyond, helping them experience the fullness of their consciousness as an endless landscape of peace, wonder, and self-discovery.

Chapter 28
Spiritual Protection

In the quiet realms of spiritual practice, where energy flows in subtle currents, practitioners recognize the need for an anchor—a source of stability and protection. This phase introduces the use of Arcturian crystals as powerful allies in spiritual protection, revealing how these sacred stones can serve as both guardians and energetic anchors, creating a resilient field around the practitioner. As the journey unfolds, safeguarding one's energetic boundaries becomes essential, and with the Arcturian crystal, practitioners find both shield and shelter.

Each crystal begins as a pristine reservoir, holding frequencies designed to harmonize and shield. Practitioners learn that these frequencies act as a fortress, forming an energetic barrier that filters and deflects disruptive vibrations. The initial steps in this practice are simple yet profound: practitioners start by choosing a crystal that resonates deeply with them, one that naturally vibrates in alignment with their energy. With this crystal, they set a clear intention for protection, allowing it to absorb and reflect their desire for safety and resilience. In this way, the crystal becomes a trusted ally, reinforcing the practitioner's energetic boundaries.

In the Ritual of Anchoring, the crystal is first placed at the center of a small, sacred space. Practitioners sit in quiet meditation, hands resting on or near the crystal, and visualize roots extending from the crystal into the earth, reaching deep into the layers below. As these roots grow, they become a grounding source, anchoring the practitioner's spirit firmly. They feel this anchor connect their own energy to the stability of the earth, creating a protective field that draws strength from the depths of the natural world.

Following the grounding ritual, practitioners move into The Sphere of Light, a visualization that envelops them in a shield of luminous energy. Holding the crystal at their heart, they begin to see a soft, radiant light expanding outward, growing from a gentle glow to a powerful, protective sphere that surrounds them completely. This sphere pulses in harmony with the crystal, filtering energies entering the practitioner's space. They sense the boundaries of this light as strong yet flexible, resilient to any disturbance, and aware of their intent to stay within this serene protection.

A deeper layer of protection is found in the Shield of Reflection exercise. Here, the practitioner holds the crystal and envisions a reflective surface around them, an invisible barrier that mirrors any disruptive energy, sending it back without absorbing it. This mirror-like shield, guided by the crystal's energy, allows only benevolent, harmonious frequencies to pass through, filtering out anything misaligned with the practitioner's energy. They become encased in an aura of gentle reflection, a boundary that remains open to positive influences but securely deflects negativity.

In the Harmonizing Aura ritual, the practitioner uses the crystal to synchronize their personal energy with a frequency of pure harmony, neutralizing any discord within or around them. Sitting with the crystal, they breathe in deeply and visualize their aura melding with the crystal's frequency. They become attuned to its protective resonance, feeling it flow through them in waves of peace, creating an internal coherence that strengthens their energetic field. This protective resonance creates a lasting shield, emanating harmony and deflecting energies that could disturb their inner calm.

The Veil of Silence introduces a silent layer of protection, a calm cloak that surrounds the practitioner, sheltering them from intrusive thoughts and emotions from the outside. In this practice, they hold the crystal at their forehead, visualizing a gentle, invisible veil descending around them. This veil dampens the energetic noise of the external world, allowing only thoughts of peace and clarity to penetrate. Practitioners feel themselves enclosed within a sanctuary of silence, where only the calmest energies can reach, fostering a quiet space for deeper reflection and spiritual focus.

For practitioners seeking an even deeper level of defense, the Shield of the Ancients brings in the wisdom of the Arcturian lineage. Practitioners visualize the crystal connecting them to an ancient lineage of spiritual protectors, energies that transcend time and space. Through the crystal, they feel the presence of these guardians, a powerful force field generated by the collective Arcturian frequency. In moments of vulnerability, they can call upon this shield, invoking the strength of this ancient energy, which stands as an unwavering barrier against any energetic intrusion.

The Breath of Purity is a powerful cleansing exercise that clears and fortifies the practitioner's energy field, using both breath and crystal energy. Holding the crystal, they breathe in deeply, feeling the crystal infuse each inhale with pure, protective energy. On the exhale, they release any tension or impurities from their field, letting them dissolve into the air. With each breath, they feel the crystal's energy filling them with clarity and resilience, creating a dynamic shield that is continuously renewed with each breath cycle, becoming ever stronger.

In The Fortress of Light, the practitioner holds the crystal in both hands, visualizing themselves encased in a fortress constructed of light—a luminous sanctuary where they are safe, secure, and free from external disturbances. This fortress is not just a defensive wall; it is a sacred space where their spiritual essence can thrive. Within this fortress, they can meditate, reflect, or simply rest, knowing they are protected. The crystal's energy supports this fortress, radiating its light outward to form a field of unwavering protection.

The Cascade of Peace brings in an element of dynamic flow, using the crystal to wash the practitioner's energy field with waves of calm, soothing any remaining disturbances. Holding the crystal at their heart, they visualize a cascade of gentle energy flowing over them, like a waterfall of light. This light washes away anything disharmonious, leaving their aura refreshed and cleansed. With each cascade, they feel their energetic boundaries reinforced, as if each drop of light strengthens the protective aura around them.

The Pillar of Eternity grounds the practitioner in a timeless protective frequency, one that is not just a temporary shield but an ongoing source of resilience. They visualize a pillar of light extending from the crystal and enveloping their entire being, connecting them to a constant flow of protective energy. This pillar creates a sense of enduring strength, a timeless space where they feel both grounded and invulnerable. It is within this pillar that the practitioner feels connected not only to their own inner power but also to the supportive presence of the greater universe.

With each of these practices, practitioners develop a personal system of protection, a series of rituals and visualizations that draw upon the unique resonance of the Arcturian crystal. These practices go beyond mere shielding—they teach the practitioner how to cultivate inner strength, resilience, and an unwavering sense of peace. Through the power of the crystal, they learn that spiritual protection is as much about nurturing their own energy as it is about deflecting unwanted influences.

In the quiet moments of these rituals, they discover the profound strength that lies within, a strength that needs no outward defense, for it is grounded in the clarity and harmony of the Arcturian frequency itself. The crystal becomes not just a shield but a partner in cultivating this inner power, a radiant guardian through which they can move freely, feeling protected, aligned, and deeply at peace with the world around them.

In the deep silence of a personal sanctuary, practitioners refine and elevate their protective energy field through advanced rituals with Arcturian crystals, accessing realms of protection that transcend the physical. Moving beyond foundational practices, this phase introduces potent techniques that strengthen the crystal's shielding power, enhancing awareness and inviting cosmic guidance to intensify the protective barrier between the practitioner and the outside world. These methods are cumulative, building one upon the other to create a deeply fortified energetic space where serenity and strength coexist.

The *Invocation of Cosmic Guardians* marks the beginning of this advanced work, connecting practitioners to energies beyond individual consciousness. Holding the crystal, they focus their intention, envisioning a radiant, protective force enveloping them, composed of benevolent guardians from higher dimensions. These cosmic entities amplify the crystal's energy, lending their wisdom to form an impenetrable shield. With the simple intention for protection, practitioners summon the guardians, who align their presence with the practitioner's energy. In this space, they are not only shielded but embraced within a cosmic web of support, each entity contributing strength to the collective barrier surrounding them.

From this strengthened field, practitioners move into The Labyrinth of Mirrors—a practice designed to deflect and diffuse any discordant energy directed toward them. Holding their crystal, they envision their protective aura transforming into a complex labyrinth, lined with mirrors that reflect and redirect any negativity. This mirrored labyrinth confuses intrusive energies, turning them away from the practitioner and back to their origin or dispersing them harmlessly into the atmosphere. Within this labyrinth, they remain untouched by outside energies, existing in a tranquil core that is wholly their own. The labyrinth becomes not only a shield but also a serene inner space, a personal sanctuary where the practitioner's energy remains entirely undisturbed.

As they deepen their connection to the crystal's energy, practitioners are introduced to The Cloak of Stars—a ritual that cloaks their aura in the vastness of cosmic energy. Visualizing their crystal as a conduit to the stars, they imagine a cloak woven from starlight descending over their shoulders, wrapping them in celestial protection. This cloak becomes a field of invisibility, blurring their energetic presence from outside perception, shielding them not just from harmful energies but also from prying attention. Within this cloak, they feel both invisible and invincible, protected by the vastness of the cosmos itself.

Another advanced technique, The Ring of Fire, draws upon the powerful transformative properties of Arcturian crystals to create a barrier of purifying energy. Sitting in meditation, they envision a ring of vibrant, ethereal fire surrounding them. This fire, fueled by the crystal's energy, does not burn; instead, it cleanses, dissolving any low-frequency energy attempting to cross its threshold. The practitioner sits safely at the center of this ring, knowing that only pure, harmonious vibrations can enter. The Ring of Fire purifies not only the surrounding space but also the practitioner's inner energy, making it both a shield and a source of ongoing renewal.

In the Echoing Silence ritual, practitioners engage with the crystal to establish a barrier of silence that reflects back any dissonance. Holding the crystal close to their heart, they visualize a wall of silent energy around them, a field that absorbs and nullifies any sound, thought, or feeling that is not aligned with peace. This barrier reflects unwanted vibrations back as an echo, sending them out into the universe where they can dissipate without impact. Within this echoing silence, practitioners find a profound peace, undisturbed by any external energy. It is a place of absolute stillness, a sanctuary of quietude where only harmonious energies may linger.

For those facing intense energetic environments, The Spiral of Resilience offers a protective method that actively strengthens the practitioner's energy. Visualizing the crystal as the core of a spiraling force, practitioners imagine a spiral of energy winding around them, wrapping them in layers of resilience. This spiral reinforces their boundaries, continuously circulating protective energy that grows stronger with each turn. As they breathe in rhythm with the spiral's motion, they feel their energy field thickening, becoming a dense yet flexible barrier. This spiral remains in place even after the meditation concludes, a lasting shield that adapts to protect them in fluctuating circumstances.

The Shield of Pure Intent aligns the crystal's protective properties with the practitioner's inner intention. Sitting in meditation with the crystal, they set a powerful intention for protection, focusing on their inner clarity and purpose. They visualize this intent filling the crystal, charging it with a specific frequency that repels all energies not aligned with their purpose. As the crystal radiates this intention outward, it becomes a shield in and of itself, a filter that only allows in energies that resonate with the practitioner's true path. This shield is particularly useful in spaces where various energies intersect, creating a selective barrier that only admits what aligns with their core intention.

In The Web of Light, the practitioner envisions a delicate, shimmering web extending from the crystal, covering their entire energy field. This web catches any discordant energy, diffusing and neutralizing it before it can touch the practitioner. Each thread of the web pulses with protective energy, forming an intricate network that is both gentle and resilient. As practitioners hold the crystal, they feel the web strengthen, its fibers tightening to block any intrusive energy. This web, though invisible to others, forms a comprehensive shield, covering even the most subtle layers of the practitioner's energy field.

For times of solitude and reflection, the Veil of Midnight offers a unique shield of quiet and detachment. Holding the crystal close, practitioners visualize a veil of midnight-blue energy covering them, allowing them to exist in a state of calm detachment from the outside world. This veil does not isolate them but instead creates a serene separation, a tranquil space that remains undisturbed by external influences. It is a protective cocoon where they can focus inward, connecting deeply with their inner guidance without distraction. Within this midnight-blue veil, they find the peace of pure solitude, a place where their own energy can breathe and expand.

The Sanctum of the Ancients takes practitioners into the deeper layers of cosmic wisdom, using the crystal to connect them with the protective knowledge of ancient energies. Holding the crystal, they visualize themselves entering a vast sanctum—a cosmic sanctuary where ancient protectors reside. These energies, timeless and wise, share their presence with the practitioner, surrounding them in an aura of immense strength and guidance. Within this sanctum, the practitioner feels shielded by the wisdom of the ages, as if the crystal itself channels the protective power of countless guardians across time and space. Here, they understand that protection is not only a barrier but a connection to the wisdom and resilience of the universe.

These advanced practices invite practitioners to engage with Arcturian crystals as partners in protection, opening pathways to higher guidance, cosmic resonance, and the depth of universal energy. Each ritual builds upon the last, creating layers of energy that are both dynamic and deeply rooted. As practitioners journey through these techniques, they discover that protection is as much about understanding the energy they wish to welcome as it is about guarding against the energies they choose to release. The Arcturian crystal becomes an ally in this balance, a guide to cultivating a space where only the purest energies can reside.

In these final practices, practitioners begin to see the crystal as a profound teacher, one that reveals the subtle art of energetic protection not only as defense but as an embrace of alignment, peace, and resilience. With each step, they become more attuned to the crystal's wisdom, realizing that true protection lies within—the quiet strength of a spirit aligned with its highest intent, shielded by both the crystal and the vast cosmos that resonates with it.

Chapter 29
Advanced Healing Techniques

In the twilight of intuitive knowing, the Arcturian crystals become like keys to a door, enabling a deeper resonance with energies that flow through the body's subtle systems. Here, practitioners explore advanced methods, using these stones not merely as tools but as intricate participants in the healing process. These techniques require not only understanding but a synchronized pulse with the crystal's unique vibrations, each carefully matched to the practitioner's healing intention. In this stage, the Arcturian crystals reveal more refined practices—ones that harmonize with the body's energy layers and move with the delicate intricacies of personal, physical, and spiritual regeneration.

A foundational practice within these advanced methods is the Harmonic Energy Grid—a complex layout combining multiple Arcturian crystals arranged according to the specific areas requiring restoration. To create the grid, practitioners begin by identifying the target energy centers or body regions in need of support, setting up each crystal to resonate with the frequencies of those particular areas. By placing each crystal with precise alignment to the body, they establish a grid that channels and amplifies energy, similar to a conductor guiding currents through a circuit. This method is particularly potent for those suffering from long-standing physical discomfort, as it allows the crystal energy to permeate deeply into tissues, cells, and energetic blocks.

Following this grid layout, practitioners engage in Cyclical Crystal Pulsing. In this practice, they work with a single crystal held close to the affected area, using breath and focus to draw in energy from the crystal in rhythmic pulses. They visualize the energy flowing through their hands, reaching the crystal, and then rebounding into the body as a pulsing wave. This pulsation aligns with natural body rhythms, such as the heartbeat, syncing with its rhythm to create an oscillating effect that promotes cellular regeneration. This technique demands focused visualization and breathwork, as the practitioner must direct their breathing to match the crystal's pulse, amplifying the restorative waves that reach the very foundation of the physical form.

To support emotional and mental healing, practitioners turn to The Web of Tranquility, a technique where multiple crystals are placed around the body in a web-like formation, typically in a sacred or serene setting. Each crystal acts as an anchor point, creating an energetic network that links to the individual's emotional layers. Visualizing each crystal as a connector within this web, practitioners focus on drawing soothing energy from each stone, feeling it gently intertwine with their own inner tensions, gradually untangling emotional knots. Through this process, they may experience a profound sense of clarity, as emotions held deep within begin to loosen, releasing old pain and replacing it with tranquility.

An advanced method known as Multi-Layer Crystal Phasing works by connecting a series of crystals, each tuned to different frequency levels—from physical to astral. Placing the stones at strategic body points, practitioners begin by focusing on the physical layer, visualizing the energy connecting to bones and muscles. As they deepen the meditation, their focus gradually ascends through the emotional, mental, and spiritual layers, feeling the energy of each crystal engaging and harmonizing with these subtler layers. This technique is designed to create multi-dimensional healing, addressing not only the body but also the invisible layers of consciousness, allowing the practitioner to emerge feeling whole on every plane.

For those seeking to clear profound blockages, Crystalline Pathways combines visualization and precise hand movements over the body's meridians, using a crystal in each hand. As they move their hands in graceful arcs along the body, practitioners visualize energy channels opening, flowing smoothly as the crystals trace these pathways. This method invokes Arcturian energy to clear energetic congestion within the meridians, restoring flow and balance. The pathways themselves feel like rivers of light, with the crystal energy easing blockages like a gentle current unfreezing ice, creating a flow that revitalizes not just the physical body but also the mind and spirit.

For practitioners ready to explore the spiritual dimensions of their energy, Celestial Crystal Alignment aligns their energy field with the higher frequencies of Arcturian consciousness. In this technique, they place crystals along their spine, from the root to the crown, and as they enter meditation, they envision each crystal connecting upward to cosmic energies. The intention is to harmonize the energy centers with celestial vibrations, allowing the energy from the Arcturian realm to descend and cleanse each center as it travels downwards. Through this alignment, they experience an influx of spiritual clarity, wisdom, and profound healing, as though their inner channels have been washed clean, leaving them open to divine insight and harmony.

A practice often employed in advanced group healing sessions is Symphonic Crystal Resonance. Here, practitioners place Arcturian crystals in a circular layout around the group, each person holding a crystal aligned with a specific need. With guided breathwork, they visualize the crystal energy amplifying into a symphony of frequencies that blend and circulate among participants. This energy flows from one person to the next, each individual's crystal resonating with the others in harmonic balance. The group setting intensifies the crystal's effects, creating a resonant field that heals collectively. Through this, practitioners experience not only personal healing but the profound interconnectedness of shared energy, each individual supporting the other in mutual restoration.

Temporal Crystal Healing, another advanced technique, is one that addresses injuries or traumas from the past that have left their imprint on the energetic body. Holding a crystal in a quiet, focused meditation, practitioners mentally journey back to the moment of the wound, visualizing the crystal energy filling the scene and shifting its frequency. As they visualize this, they bring light and understanding to the moment, allowing the Arcturian energy to cleanse and heal it. They may notice feelings of release, as though the energy of that memory has shifted, allowing it to integrate peacefully into the present without the weight of pain or resistance.

In The Lattice of Unity, practitioners integrate several crystals along the body's chakras to create a grid that harmonizes both the physical and spiritual planes. Laying in a meditative position, they place stones on each energy center, feeling the lattice connect from the root to the crown. This crystal lattice strengthens unity between body and spirit, creating a profound sense of interconnectedness within. As they breathe, they feel the energy moving smoothly along the lattice, each chakra attuned to its corresponding crystal, and an overarching sense of cohesion fills their body, bringing peace and oneness.

Through each of these techniques, the practitioner advances in their understanding of Arcturian crystals as co-creators in the healing journey. These stones serve not only as sources of energy but as guides, gently leading the practitioner deeper into the fabric of their own being. In each practice, the body, mind, and spirit are touched, and with every session, practitioners learn that healing is as much about reconnecting with their own energy's depth as it is about aligning with the vast support offered by the crystals. The Arcturian frequency, woven into each stone, reveals itself as a quiet, powerful current, flowing through and transforming the practitioner, layer by layer.

In the depths of advanced healing, the Arcturian crystals emerge not only as conduits of energy but as powerful entities capable of reshaping the subtleties of the human spirit and the body's most intricate layers. Practitioners who reach this level of understanding are ready to work beyond traditional methods, aligning themselves with energies that resonate at the threshold of the mystical. Here, the crystals become more than tools; they become allies, each interaction between crystal and practitioner an unspoken exchange of ancient knowledge, an invitation to reach beyond the physical into the profound.

The journey begins with Layered Frequency Tuning, a technique that draws on the resonance of multiple crystals layered in succession over the body, creating a cascading flow of energies. Each crystal is selected to vibrate at a slightly different frequency, attuned to a particular layer within the practitioner's energetic field, from the dense and physical to the ethereal and spiritual. In this arrangement, the crystals act like steps on an energy staircase, guiding the practitioner upward, layer by layer, helping them peel away embedded energetic blocks or stagnant emotions as they ascend.

In tandem with this is Time-Loop Energy Release, a method rooted in shifting repetitive energetic patterns and ancient karmic imprints. Here, the practitioner uses crystals to form an energetic loop around the self, holding one crystal in each hand while envisioning a cycle of energy flowing in a loop around them, carrying with it remnants of the past or self-imposed barriers. As they breathe, they begin to dissolve these patterns, observing any sensations, memories, or images that surface as the loop grows fainter. This process allows a release that is both deeply personal and, often, subtly transformative, loosening energetic binds that may have persisted across lifetimes.

In the space where the mind meets the spirit, Transmutational Crystal Fusion calls upon the crystals' Arcturian essence to facilitate a fusion of energies within the chakras. Beginning at the heart, the practitioner places a crystal on each major chakra point, visualizing the merging of each center's energy with the crystal's own light. Through this integration, the practitioner opens pathways for deeper alignment with their higher self, removing any stagnant shadows that might cling to these centers. With each chakra merged with crystal energy, there is a gradual but undeniable shift in the energy body, as though it is fine-tuned to a higher pitch, in sync with its true frequency.

In the practice of Crystalline Temporal Cleansing, the crystals act as gateways through which the practitioner can cleanse specific life phases. Holding an Arcturian crystal, they meditate on a particular period in their past, visualizing the crystal filling this time with its own light, cleansing any lingering disturbances or energetic residues left by unresolved events or memories. By focusing on the release of these energies within the crystal's light, the practitioner becomes free of the emotional weight of those memories. As each layer is stripped away, there is a sensation of lightness, of burdens removed, leaving the practitioner open to the present moment, unshackled from the weight of history.

For emotional release and expansion, practitioners can use The Crystal Spiral Flow, a method that requires an intricate positioning of crystals in a spiral formation on the practitioner's back or solar plexus, representing the unfolding path of personal evolution. The energy of the spiral is believed to draw out hidden aspects of the self, whether dormant desires, unspoken fears, or deeply buried aspirations, and release them gently into consciousness. As they lie within the spiral, practitioners may feel their emotions emerge and dissipate, giving them a profound sense of freedom from the labyrinth of their inner landscape.

In advanced group healings, Unified Frequency Resonance brings multiple practitioners together in an intricate formation, with each holding an Arcturian crystal specific to their own intention or need. Arranged in a circle, they focus on sending their energy into their crystal, while synchronizing their breath with those around them. The energy shared between each practitioner is amplified through the crystals, creating a unified resonance that becomes a powerful healing force. This shared frequency resonates not only within each individual but also as a collective vibration that can touch the larger space they occupy, fostering both personal and shared healing in an environment of trust and unity.

The Veil of Transition technique is one that resonates with the realms beyond physical perception. Here, practitioners prepare for times of significant transition—such as letting go of a role, embracing change, or making a leap in spiritual awareness. With a crystal placed on the third eye and another on the solar plexus, they meditate on the phase they are moving from, feeling the crystal draw out attachments, fears, or doubts. Visualizing the crystal as a bridge, they walk mentally from the past phase to the next, feeling the crystal's energies support each step. With each inhalation, they sense that which is necessary and beneficial, bringing it forward into the present, and each exhale releases all that hinders.

Practitioners exploring the broader energies of their spiritual journey turn to Celestial Channeling, a technique wherein the crystals are arranged above the crown chakra in a half-circle, forming a portal to the Arcturian frequency. In this meditative state, practitioners hold the intention of connecting with a higher plane, feeling the crystal's light create a channel that extends beyond time and space, touching the Arcturian essence. Through this, they may experience insights, messages, or symbols that emerge from the silence, carried through the crystal's resonance, offering them guidance or answers to their deepest questions. Often, these insights take the form of gentle knowing rather than direct thoughts, as though an ancient wisdom flows wordlessly through the practitioner's awareness.

In Soul Matrix Rejuvenation, crystals are placed in a series along the spine, each connected to a different aspect of the practitioner's soul journey. Through breath and visualization, practitioners align each crystal to a facet of their soul's essence, such as creativity, purpose, or connection to the divine. This connection brings a refreshing energy flow, as though recharging each part of their soul, enhancing clarity and vitality in daily life. As they move through the visualization, they may feel the energy realigning their perception, their thoughts attuned once more to the frequency of their soul's purpose.

For those attuned to the subtle rhythms of the earth, Earth Harmonic Attunement uses a selection of crystals placed around the body to match the resonance of the earth's energetic grid. Lying with these crystals at specific energy points (such as hands, feet, and heart), the practitioner feels the grounding and stabilizing force of the earth's rhythms flowing through each crystal. This practice opens channels to both receive and transmit energy back to the earth, creating a symbiotic relationship. Often, practitioners will feel a rooted sense of connection, as though held by the earth itself, absorbing and sharing energy that is both nourishing and steadying.

The Arcturian crystals, in their clarity and strength, offer practitioners a means of engaging with their own depth and potential in ways they may have never before experienced. Each technique illuminates new avenues of self-awareness, from the microscopic sensations within the body to the transcendent energies that brush the soul's outermost edges. Working with these crystals becomes a sacred ritual, a communion of energy and intent that brings practitioners to the brink of personal discovery. The journey through these advanced techniques is not just a practice in healing; it is a dance with the energy of life itself, in a rhythm that grows ever more harmonious with each step.

Chapter 30
Personal Journey

The personal journey through the lens of Arcturian crystals begins with a profound sense of invitation, as though each crystal beckons the practitioner to step deeper into the landscape of their own soul. This path, however, is not linear or predictable. It unfolds in spirals and layers, where each discovery is met with new questions, and every revelation gently peels back yet another veil of the self. As practitioners embark on this inward voyage, the crystals serve as steadfast guides, amplifying clarity, providing grounding, and revealing inner truths. In their presence, the journey becomes both a map and a mirror, guiding the practitioner to see not only where they have been but also the potential of where they are destined to go.

A significant first step in this exploration is the Intention of Alignment. To engage deeply, practitioners begin by holding a crystal close to their heart, feeling its steady vibration align with their heartbeat. In this moment, they set an intention—whether it is to gain insight, release old patterns, or open themselves to growth. The crystal acts as an anchor for this intention, creating a sacred promise to oneself and a reminder of the commitment to grow. Through this simple act, the practitioner tunes into their soul's frequency, connecting with their inner compass and finding the courage to move forward into self-exploration.

The path forward often leads to Inner Terrain Mapping. Here, the crystal acts as a subtle illuminator, guiding the practitioner to parts of the self that may have gone unexplored or were perhaps forgotten. Holding the crystal in a meditative state, they move their awareness throughout their own body, emotions, and thoughts, sensing areas of ease and areas of resistance. The crystal serves as a gentle but unyielding light, shining into pockets of hidden fears, unvoiced desires, and fragments of dreams long held in secret. As they breathe, the practitioner begins to visualize this terrain with newfound clarity, allowing them to navigate both the bright and shadowed aspects of their personal landscape with acceptance.

In these early stages, there is an inevitable meeting with Echoes of the Past. The crystal becomes a bridge between time, drawing memories or past emotional patterns into the present, allowing the practitioner to witness their own history from a place of clarity and compassion. Cradling the crystal, the practitioner may sit in silent reflection, inviting any memories or insights that arise to come forth. Whether they are moments of joy, regret, or transformation, each memory is acknowledged and released into the crystal's energy. Through this process, the practitioner begins to untangle from the threads of the past, honoring each experience while setting themselves free from its lingering influence.

As the journey progresses, the crystal's role deepens, guiding the practitioner into Harmonizing Self-Truths. This stage invites an honest dialogue with oneself—questions of identity, purpose, and authenticity arise, asking to be heard. With the crystal as a focal point, the practitioner engages in quiet contemplation, examining the beliefs they hold about themselves and the lives they have chosen. They may feel a heightened sensitivity to what resonates as true and what feels like remnants of another's influence. This stage can bring a sense of profound liberation, as the crystal amplifies the clarity needed to stand firmly in one's own truth, shedding all that feels misaligned with their core essence.

Through these revelations, there arises the desire for Crystalline Affirmation Practices. These practices are simple yet powerful affirmations that solidify the practitioner's personal insights and intentions. By holding the crystal and speaking or mentally affirming chosen phrases—such as "I trust my path," or

"I honor my inner wisdom"—they infuse these words into the crystal's energy field. This act creates a living, vibrational reminder of their commitment to themselves, with each affirmation resonating back to them whenever they hold or work with the crystal again. In this way, the crystal becomes both an external guide and a keeper of the practitioner's truths, grounding their evolving self-perception.

In some cases, the journey requires a focus on Releasing Self-Imposed Limitations. The crystal here serves as a catalyst, helping to identify and gently dismantle self-imposed barriers and limiting beliefs that may have accumulated over time. In a meditative state, the practitioner holds the crystal at their solar plexus, visualizing it absorbing any beliefs or thoughts that inhibit growth or reinforce doubt. As these limitations are gathered, the crystal's energy works to dissolve them, filling the practitioner with a renewed sense of freedom and possibility. By lifting these self-imposed restrictions, they open to the broader scope of their own potential.

At this juncture, there is a subtle shift toward Dream and Vision Pathwork, where the crystal guides the practitioner to envision the life they wish to create. This visioning process is not a mere exercise in daydreaming; rather, it is a heartfelt connection with one's deepest aspirations. With the crystal held at the third eye, the practitioner begins to visualize scenarios, environments, or qualities that embody their soul's desires. Through the crystal's guidance, they allow these images to crystallize within their mind, shaping a pathway forward. This visioning practice fosters clarity, imbuing the practitioner with a tangible sense of direction and purpose, as though glimpsing fragments of a future already waiting to be embraced.

To aid in moments of doubt or challenge along the path, the practitioner is encouraged to engage in Crystalline Resilience Techniques. These techniques are designed to foster inner strength, patience, and faith during times of uncertainty. By holding the crystal close to the heart and visualizing its light spreading throughout the body, the practitioner connects with a reservoir of inner resilience. Each inhale draws in courage, while each exhale releases worry or fear, creating an energetic shield that protects the practitioner's sense of purpose even in turbulent moments. The crystal thus becomes a symbol of unwavering support, a reminder of the practitioner's ability to persist, no matter the obstacles.

In the silence of these experiences, there lies a powerful practice known as Echoes of Potential. Here, the crystal is placed near the root chakra, inviting visions or sensations connected to untapped potential or inner talents yet undiscovered. This practice is not so much about searching but allowing—letting the crystal's energy awaken dormant skills or desires that lie just below the surface. Practitioners may find themselves drawn to explore unfamiliar paths, new creative endeavors, or rediscover long-abandoned passions, each emerging with a quiet certainty as though remembering an ancient aspect of themselves. Through this resonance, the crystal reminds them of the vast capacity within, waiting patiently for expression.

In the journey's gradual unfolding, the practice of Daily Gratitude Imbuement becomes a way to honor each step taken. At the end of each day, the practitioner holds the crystal, reflecting on any insights, lessons, or experiences gained, no matter how small. With each expression of gratitude, they breathe this feeling into the crystal, creating an ongoing resonance of appreciation that grows with time. This imbued energy of gratitude helps to sustain the practitioner, transforming the crystal into a wellspring of encouragement that they can return to in moments of need, drawing from its energy of fulfillment and contentment.

As the crystal holds space for all these stages, it becomes more than a tool; it is a companion on the personal journey, a constant source of wisdom, and a witness to transformation. Each step forward is not just a step toward external goals but a movement closer to the self, toward a truer understanding of one's essence and purpose. The path of the personal journey is winding and sometimes shadowed, yet with each glimmer of the crystal's light, practitioners find the strength to step deeper into the mystery, knowing that their soul's unfolding is a treasure uniquely their own.

In the journey toward self-discovery, there exists a subtle shift as one moves from exploration into integration. Within the energy of the Arcturian crystal, this transition becomes a dance between the known and unknown, where newfound insights and revelations no longer exist as abstract thoughts but as lived realities. Here, the practitioner begins to embody the changes uncovered in the first steps of the personal journey, weaving them deeply into their everyday experience. The crystal, ever a guide, assists in this process, helping to anchor growth into the foundation of daily life, ensuring that each insight strengthens the core of the practitioner's being.

This part of the journey begins with Soul Anchoring Practices, where the practitioner uses the crystal to ground the insights gained so far. Sitting in a quiet, reflective space, the practitioner places the crystal near the root chakra, visualizing a steady energy flowing from it, rooting deeply into the Earth. As they breathe, they allow each revelation, each lesson, to settle within them, grounding these changes like roots of an ancient tree. This act of anchoring is not simply about stability but about presence—a commitment to live each day as an extension of the truths they have uncovered.

As these truths take root, the practitioner moves into Reflective Crystalline Journaling. With the crystal close by, they write freely, recording thoughts, feelings, and emerging questions. The crystal serves as a focal point for clarity, aiding in the discernment of what resonates deeply and what echoes as fleeting distractions. Through this reflective practice, insights become more than passing thoughts; they are written into the narrative of the practitioner's life. Each entry holds the power to reveal recurring themes, subtle nudges from the soul, guiding the practitioner to honor the journey with intention and awareness.

In alignment with this introspective practice, the path reveals the need for Creating Soul-Aligned Intentions. Here, the practitioner revisits goals, not as external aspirations but as reflections of their innermost values and desires. Holding the crystal, they begin to set intentions that are deeply aligned with their personal journey. Whether the focus is on creativity, self-acceptance, or purposeful living, these intentions serve as markers along the path, each one a quiet promise to remain true to the evolving self. With each intention, the crystal amplifies the energy, creating a resonance that both attracts and sustains alignment.

With these intentions comes the opportunity for Conscious Daily Practices, subtle rituals that bring these inner transformations into daily life. The practitioner selects small actions, such as morning reflections or mindful breathing with the crystal, that remind them of their journey. These practices become quiet touchstones throughout the day, providing moments of pause and realignment. In these brief connections, the crystal acts as a conduit, infusing each practice with the essence of their journey, ensuring that each action, no matter how routine, becomes part of the soul's unfolding.

As the journey continues, there emerges a need for Receptivity to Inner Whispers. With the crystal held at the heart, the practitioner quiets their mind, creating a space to listen—not to thoughts, but to the subtle, gentle whispers of intuition. These whispers, often quiet and unassuming, hold the essence of guidance. The crystal amplifies these inner voices, allowing the practitioner to receive insights that may otherwise go unnoticed. In these moments, the practitioner becomes both listener and witness, aware that the guidance they seek often exists within, waiting for them to become still enough to hear.

In time, the practitioner is drawn to Recognizing and Celebrating Personal Growth. Holding the crystal, they take a moment to acknowledge the progress made, not in grand gestures but in the small, subtle shifts that often go uncelebrated. By honoring these moments, they create a sense of gratitude, filling the crystal with the energy of self-appreciation and respect for the journey. This act of celebration is not only for the past but a way to energize future steps, instilling each one with a sense of purpose and joy, knowing that every part of the path holds value.

The journey's progression naturally brings forward the practice of Releasing External Expectations. In a meditative state, the practitioner holds the crystal, reflecting on the influences and opinions that have shaped them. They observe which expectations feel genuine and which feel imposed. Through this quiet reflection, the crystal aids in gently releasing any energies or beliefs that no longer serve. This release opens the space to cultivate authenticity, allowing the practitioner to engage in life from a place of truth rather than obligation.

From this space of clarity, the path turns toward Cultivating Inner Harmony. The practitioner holds the crystal, drawing upon its calming energy to balance the shifts within. With each breath, they harmonize the energies of mind, body, and spirit, ensuring that each part of the self resonates with the path ahead. The crystal serves as a stabilizing force, creating a foundation where all aspects of the self are in unity, no part overshadowing another. This harmony fosters resilience, helping the practitioner to move forward with peace, even amidst life's ebbs and flows.

In moments of challenge, the practitioner may engage in Crystalline Resilience Visualization. Here, they visualize the crystal expanding in light, creating a sphere of resilience around them. This visualization strengthens their energetic field, allowing them to navigate difficulties with a sense of calm and confidence. The crystal acts as both shield and guide, reminding them that each challenge is but a part of the journey, and within them lies the capacity to persevere.

The journey's culmination arrives in the form of Integration into Wholeness. At this stage, the practitioner holds the crystal, acknowledging that every experience, every insight, has brought them closer to their essence. In this quiet, sacred moment, they recognize that they are both the seeker and the wisdom they sought. The crystal, now an extension of their journey, serves as a reminder of their path, a symbol of the self that has emerged through each step. As they close their eyes, they feel a sense of completion—not as an end, but as a state of becoming, knowing that this journey is ever-evolving, an endless unfolding into deeper layers of the self.

Chapter 31
Crystal Integration

After traversing the depths of personal transformation, healing, and alignment, the journey begins to circle back upon itself, returning not to a starting point but to a newfound center. Here, the crystal is no longer just a tool or guide; it becomes an integral part of daily life, woven into the very fabric of the practitioner's routine. In this phase of crystal integration, the practitioner reaches a stage of wholeness, where the energies, insights, and revelations are absorbed, understood, and lived without effort. The crystal, now a companion and mirror of this expanded state, supports the seamless flow of Arcturian energy into the daily experience.

To anchor this phase, the practitioner begins with Morning Connection Rituals. Each morning, they hold the crystal close, breathing deeply and allowing its energy to permeate the senses, mind, and heart. These moments of quiet connection are neither structured nor ritualistic in the traditional sense but are rather gentle reminders to open to the crystal's resonance as a part of the day's energy. The crystal's presence becomes a grounding force, aligning the day with clarity, focus, and tranquility. By starting with this calm connection, the practitioner feels the flow of Arcturian energy guiding them with subtle strength and balance throughout the day.

Building upon this is the practice of Mindful Energy Tuning. As life continues with its inherent pace and occasional challenges, the practitioner learns to check in with their energetic alignment frequently, using the crystal as a tuning device. This could mean carrying the crystal close by, perhaps in a pocket or worn as a pendant, and pausing periodically to feel its vibration. With each pause, the practitioner notices areas of imbalance, tension, or scattered thoughts and uses the crystal to bring harmony back to these spaces. This tuning is as natural as breathing and grows to become a seamless, almost subconscious habit, integrating harmony into the fabric of everyday existence.

The practitioner is also introduced to Home Energy Harmonization. By now, the crystal has extended its resonance beyond personal energy, and its influence expands to the physical space the practitioner inhabits. In a conscious practice, the practitioner places crystals throughout their home to maintain a continuous flow of Arcturian energy. Whether set by windows to absorb sunlight, by doors to protect and welcome, or near spaces dedicated to relaxation, each crystal serves a distinct purpose, creating a sanctuary that resonates with the practitioner's energy. This arrangement becomes a silent guardian, holding space for peace, clarity, and renewal throughout the environment.

A powerful component of integration lies in Sacred Moments of Gratitude. At various times throughout the day—whether during transitions, after a meaningful conversation, or in moments of stillness—the practitioner holds the crystal and reflects on the journey it has enabled. These reflections are more than gratitude; they are recognitions of the crystal's role as a steadfast companion, silently amplifying each step toward alignment, healing, and transformation. These moments deepen the connection, infusing the crystal with gratitude while affirming its role as a lifelong partner in this spiritual journey.

Another essential practice in this stage of integration is Crystal-Infused Intentions for Daily Actions. Here, the practitioner begins to infuse their actions, no matter how small, with the intentions held within the crystal. From a simple interaction to complex tasks, the crystal's energy is called upon to imbue each action with clarity, compassion, or resilience, depending on the need. This integration brings a mindful approach to life, where the practitioner consciously chooses how they wish to show up in each moment, guided by the crystal's quiet but potent influence.

As integration deepens, the practitioner explores Evening Reflection with the Crystal. In this time, they hold the crystal and reflect on the day's moments of alignment and dissonance, acknowledging how the crystal's presence has woven through each experience. This reflection is less about analyzing and more about gently observing, allowing the crystal to absorb the day's energies and help the practitioner release any tensions, doubts, or lingering attachments. This evening ritual creates a sense of closure, preparing the mind and spirit to rest with peace and clarity, carrying no energetic residue into the realm of sleep.

Integration also involves recognizing the crystal's presence in Creative Expansion. The practitioner begins to notice that the crystal's energy does not remain static but grows, amplifying their creative expression. Whether through art, writing, or problem-solving, the crystal supports the mind's capacity to envision and create, tapping into the Arcturian frequency's unique inspiration. The crystal's presence dissolves creative blocks, allowing the practitioner to explore new ideas and solutions with ease, guided by an intuitive flow that feels almost like a whisper from the crystal itself.

In the course of this process, the practitioner embraces Living with Purposeful Simplicity. With the crystal integrated fully, the practitioner is less drawn to complexities and finds a deep satisfaction in simplicity. Each day's rhythm becomes a quiet reflection of their alignment, infused with purpose but free of unnecessary complications. The crystal's energy clears distractions, drawing attention back to what truly resonates with the practitioner's heart and purpose. This simplicity becomes a source of inner peace, as the crystal's resonance supports the clarity needed to let go of what does not serve.

To further deepen this phase, the practitioner learns Adaptable Crystal Connection. The crystal now feels like an extension of the self, and the practitioner no longer needs to schedule specific practices or rituals. Instead, they develop a fluid and adaptable connection, sensing intuitively when they need to engage with the crystal's energy. This fluidity is the essence of integration; the crystal's guidance is not a separate practice but a natural aspect of the practitioner's awareness. Whether at a moment of decision, in a period of rest, or amid a busy day, the crystal's presence is felt, its energy always accessible and adaptive.

As the practice unfolds, the practitioner encounters *Transcending Dependency on the Crystal*. In this ultimate stage of integration, they realize the crystal's purpose was never to create dependency but to lead them toward a state of inner sovereignty. The crystal has been a guide, a support, a mirror, but ultimately, its energy now reflects the inner strength, wisdom, and harmony the practitioner has cultivated within themselves. Holding the crystal one last time in this practice, they acknowledge it as a friend, an ally in the journey, yet now also recognize the boundless reservoir of Arcturian energy they hold within their own spirit.

In these practices, the integration process completes not as an ending, but as a reminder of the interconnectedness between the crystal, the self, and the journey. As each moment, thought, and action aligns with this expanded awareness, the crystal's role shifts, moving into the background like a gentle pulse—a silent testament to the journey from discovery to integration, from separation to unity.

As the integration journey continues, the crystal becomes more than a spiritual ally; it evolves into a subtle yet constant presence in the practitioner's life, silently amplifying a state of peace, insight, and connection. In this final phase, the practice reaches a state of completion, where the crystal's energy is fully internalized, and the practitioner exists in harmonious flow with the Arcturian frequency. This is not a conclusion but a beginning—a deep immersion into a lifestyle shaped by the qualities of balance, resilience, and wisdom that the crystal has fostered.

The practitioner now explores Living in Resonance. Here, the Arcturian crystal's energy becomes so intertwined with the practitioner's vibration that they exist in a state of continuous resonance, unaffected by external disturbances. Life's challenges still arise, but they no longer unsettle the practitioner's equilibrium. Instead, they are met with a calm and grounded awareness, the crystal's energy reinforcing the understanding that true strength lies in fluidity and acceptance. The practitioner learns to remain attuned to this harmony, recognizing that their inner peace shapes the external experience.

In this phase, The Path of Self-Awareness deepens, and the crystal serves as a tool of self-reflection. The practitioner can hold the crystal in moments of contemplation, allowing it to amplify clarity and highlight any unacknowledged patterns or hidden aspects of the self. This practice unveils the layers of self, drawing attention to thoughts, habits, or beliefs that may have gone unnoticed, fostering a gentle process of self-discovery and alignment. The crystal's energy helps dissolve old attachments, encouraging a state of being that is flexible, open, and deeply attuned to growth.

Building on this awareness, the practitioner now practices Effortless Intuition. By this stage, intuition flows naturally, guided by the crystal's subtle influence on the third eye. Decisions, once questioned and pondered, now emerge from a quiet place of inner knowing, a voice that does not need analysis or proof. The crystal's energy refines the practitioner's ability to perceive truth and to trust it, dissolving fears and doubts. This effortless intuition shapes each day's rhythm, guiding choices that align seamlessly with the practitioner's true path, as if each step is lit by a gentle yet unwavering light.

The crystal's presence also evolves into Guiding Dreams and Visions. As sleep deepens into a more receptive state, the crystal's energy begins to permeate dreams, enabling a form of communication from deeper realms. These dreams are not always vivid but carry a sense of guidance and clarity upon waking. Some dreams might reveal insights about the journey ahead, while others offer resolutions to past or present matters. The practitioner may keep the crystal near during sleep, inviting its energy into these nighttime journeys, feeling supported by the Arcturian frequency even as they explore the subconscious mind.

As the integration process matures, the practitioner embraces Shared Energy Practices. This is where the crystal's energy, now deeply familiar, can be consciously extended toward others in need. Without imposing, the practitioner learns to share the crystal's energy, sending compassion, healing, or protection as needed. This is done with mindful intent, a silent practice where the practitioner draws upon the Arcturian frequency within the crystal, radiating it outwards to comfort, soothe, or uplift others. The crystal becomes a vessel of shared purpose, connecting the practitioner's life with those around them.

In daily life, the practitioner continues with Effortless Presence. The crystal's energy promotes a mindful state in every interaction, in every step, in each breath. It draws the practitioner's awareness to the present moment, grounding them in the simplicity of now. No matter the task, the practitioner's presence feels centered and purposeful, guided by the crystal's energy that radiates as an ever-present reminder to live fully. There is no hurry, no resistance—only a natural flow from one experience to the next, each moment honored as part of a greater whole.

Another profound transformation unfolds in the form of Enduring Strength in Solitude. The practitioner finds a quiet joy in solitude, where the crystal's energy supports a deep connection with the self, unclouded by external influences. The crystal's energy resonates with a profound inner strength, encouraging the practitioner to embrace their unique path, unshaken by opinions, expectations, or external noise. Through this, solitude transforms from mere absence of company to a sanctuary of self-discovery, where the practitioner finds peace, strength, and inspiration, knowing that the crystal's energy will always illuminate this journey.

The practitioner also discovers the power of Surrendering Control. Here, they release the need to guide or plan each step, trusting the Arcturian energy that flows through the crystal and themselves. This surrender is not passive but a deep form of trust, allowing life to unfold in its own rhythm, assured that they are held within a field of protection and guidance. The crystal becomes a reminder of this surrender, showing that the essence of spiritual growth lies in allowing rather than forcing, in embracing rather than resisting.

In moments of contemplation, the practitioner engages in Unified Alignment with the Universe. With the crystal in hand, they feel their energy merge with the cosmos, recognizing the oneness of all life. This alignment offers insights beyond the self, drawing the practitioner's awareness to the subtle interconnections that weave through existence. This deep state of alignment reveals how their journey, though personal, is a thread in the vast tapestry of universal consciousness, connected and contributing to a greater purpose.

In these final stages of integration, the practitioner reaches Eternal Reflection and Renewal. With the crystal as a constant companion, the practitioner's journey becomes one of continuous growth. The crystal's energy no longer marks stages of progress but an eternal cycle of reflection, renewal, and realization. The practitioner views life as a sacred journey, a practice where the boundaries between self, crystal, and cosmos dissolve, blending into an infinite flow of consciousness. The crystal serves as a mirror in this journey, reflecting both the practitioner's essence and the limitless energy of the universe itself.

In this ultimate state, the practitioner experiences Self as a Living Crystal. They feel an internal crystallization, where their energy resonates in harmony with the Arcturian frequency as if they have become a crystal themselves. Just as the crystal channels, protects, and heals, so too does the practitioner radiate qualities of clarity, resilience, and healing energy. This self-crystallization represents the culmination of their journey, a testament to the depths they have explored, the transformations they have embraced, and the wisdom they now carry forward.

Thus, the journey of crystal integration completes, not as a linear path but as a profound return to unity. The crystal, now inseparable from the practitioner's essence, continues to resonate as a silent guide, a reminder of the boundless depths of consciousness and the infinite power within. Each moment, each breath, carries the whisper of the crystal's energy, gently guiding the practitioner into a life lived with grace, peace, and a timeless connection to the Arcturian frequency that will forever illuminate their path.

Epilogue

At the end of this journey, the silence now permeating your being carries a new type of understanding. A clarity that is not born of rational comprehension but of a lived experience, felt in the deepest layers of your spirit. The energy that has passed through each crystal has also touched your heart, like a silent guide revealing, subtly, the secrets that have always awaited. And what has been awakened in you does not vanish but transforms into a point of reference, an internal space where peace and clarity can be accessed at any moment.

This experience of opening yourself to the resonance of these crystals is an ongoing journey. It is a process of refinement, an invitation to revisit what was learned and perceive how the frequency that once seemed external now pulses within you. The Arcturians, with their protective and harmonizing energy, have left invisible marks on your field, resonances that have strengthened not only your spirit but your perception of reality. Now, more than ever, you can recognize this peace, feel the power of an energy that demands nothing but offers everything.

This bond you have built is enduring. Just as the crystals hold the Arcturian frequency within, you now carry this connection within your own energy field as an anchor of serenity amid life's fluctuations. The external world may still challenge and demand, but the difference lies in how you stand firm. Like a polished crystal, your energy now shines, ready to absorb what strengthens and reflect what is unnecessary.

The Arcturians, through these crystals, have taught you the subtlety of existing in harmony with the universe. Now, each breath is a reminder that you are part of this vastness, that there is always a space of light that welcomes and sustains you. They have shown you that true protection comes from understanding who you are and from the capacity to harmonize with the forces that sustain all life.

This learning is a quietly growing seed, and you realize it has no end. Each future interaction with these crystals will bring new layers of understanding, new ways of seeing and feeling. They become not only allies but reflections of what is pure and true within you. They are portals to a state of consciousness where time and space are merely details, where true power lies in peace.

Every moment you return to these crystals, feeling their presence, you also return to that part of yourself that knows the way, that aligns with the frequency of peace, healing, balance. This journey of self-discovery and expansion does not end here. It extends each day, in every breath, in the quiet of knowing that you carry within you the frequency of the universe, in harmony and protected, always.

www.ingramcontent.com/pod-product-compliance
Lightning Source LLC
LaVergne TN
LVHW040049080526
838202LV00045B/3551